Sources of

Economic Information:

Ireland

Second edition, revised and updated

Renuka Page

Institute of Public Administration

First published 1985
Second edition revised and updated 1999
by the Institute of Public Administration
57-61 Lansdowne Road, Dublin 4, Ireland
www.ipa.ie

© 1985, 1999 Renuka Page

British Library Cataloguing-in-Publication Data
A catalogue record for this book is available from
the British Library.

ISBN 1 902448 07 3

Typeset in 9/10 Times New Roman by Anne Mc
Entee Typesetting & Design, Drogheda and printed
by ColourBooks Ltd, Dublin.

Contents

Acknowledgements

I wish to express my gratitude and thanks to Professor John FitzGerald, Economic and Social Research Institute, for reading through my manuscript and for his comments and suggestions.

For giving me access to the holdings of their libraries, I am much obliged to Eileen McGlade, Trinity College Dublin; Tim Kelly, European Communities Office; Deirdre Brennan, Teagasc; Sarah Burns, Economic and Social Research Institute; Catherine Dempsey, Central Statistics Office, Mairéad Ní Bhriain, Central Bank of Ireland; Mary Doyle, Department of Agriculture and Food; Linda Hamilton, Electricity Supply Board; Sharon McGrath, Department of the Marine and Natural Resources, Forest Service.

My thanks to Tony McNamara of the Institute of Public Administration, my publisher.

A special thanks to Brendan O'Brien for his painstaking copy-editing and to Anne Mc Entee for her professional typesetting service.

Introduction

A vast amount of economic information on Ireland is contained in a wide range of documents published by the Central Statistics Office, Government Departments, Committees, Commissions, Councils, research institutions, societies, State-sponsored bodies, banks, international organisations, commercial and professional organisations. Many of these documents overlap, and the information contained in some is derived from information contained in others. This book is a guide to these documents.

Arrangement
There are 19 sections. The documents dealt with in each section are arranged in the following order:
>	Official Publications
>	Other Publications: Irish
>	Other Publications: British
>	Publications: International Organisations.

Within each category documents are listed alphabetically by corporate author.

All entries are indexed by corporate author, title and subject.

Scope and coverage
Only current documents are included. A brief summary is given of the information contained in each document, but no attempt is made to analyse or evaluate this information.

The only Acts of the Oireachtas covered in this source book are the Finance Acts.

Journal articles have not been indexed.

Agriculture, Fisheries & Forestry

Official Publications

Central Statistics Office
CENSUS OF AGRICULTURE
Dublin: Central Statistics Office (periodically)

The *Census of Agriculture June 1991: detailed results*, published in May 1994, was the first full census to be conducted since 1980. Censuses had previously been conducted at five-yearly intervals since 1960 and annually between 1847 and 1953 inclusive.

These censuses provide, for each county and rural district, details of land usage and the numbers of cattle and sheep. They also contain, for each county, details of the number and the size of agricultural holdings, numbers of other livestock and certain items of agricultural machinery, as well as the area of land let for tillage and grazing.

The 45 tables include:

- number of farms classified by farm size in each province and county
- number of farms classified by farm size and by type of farm
- number of family farms classified by characteristics of holder and by type of farm
- number of farms growing crops and the area of crops in each province and county
- farms growing cereals classified by farm size and area under cereals
- farms with cattle, sheep or pigs classified by farm size and size of herd
- number of farms involved in organic farming in each province and county.

Central Statistics Office
ECONOMIC SERIES
Dublin: Stationery Office (monthly)

The *Economic Series* bulletin provides up-to-date information and five years' retrospection for a selection of 151 principal short-term economic series. Longer retrospection is given in each December issue.
　　Charts and graphs accompany the tables. The numbers pertaining to agriculture are:

4.01	Exports of cattle
4.02	Number of cattle slaughtered
4.03	Number of pigs slaughtered
4.04	Number of sheep slaughtered
4.05	Milk intake.

Central Statistics Office
STATISTICAL ABSTRACT
Dublin: Stationery Office (annually)

Each issue of the *Statistical Abstract* contains a section on Agriculture, Forestry and Fisheries. The tables are supported by an explanatory text and are divided into various sections. Examples from the 1996 *Statistical Abstract* are listed below.

1

Crops and livestock
- estimated area, yield and production of crops, 1991–1995
- area under crops and pasture in June
- number of cattle and sheep in June
- estimated number of livestock in December

Land sales
- agricultural land sales

Labour
- agricultural labour input (persons)
- agricultural labour input (annual work units)

Agricultural wages
- minimum rates of wages of agricultural workers
- average minimum weekly rates and index numbers of wages of permanent agricultural workers

Agricultural output
- estimated quantity of agricultural output
- estimated value of agricultural output
- estimated output, input and income in agriculture
- output of cattle and calves – estimated number
- output of cattle and calves – estimated value
- output of pigs, sheep and lambs – estimated number and value
- milk output and disposal (whole milk only)

Livestock improvements

Forestry
Coillte Teoranta owned forest properties

Fisheries
- quantity of sea fish (excluding salmon) returned as landed by Irish-registered vessels into Irish ports
- value of sea fish returned as landed by Irish-registered vessels into Irish ports
- catches of inland fish
- persons engaged in sea fishing

Central Statistics Office
STATISTICAL BULLETIN + Index
Dublin: Stationery Office (quarterly)

The *Statistical Bulletin* is one of the principal sources of information on Irish agriculture. Text and tables provide this information under various headings, as follows.

Agricultural statistics
- land utilisation and number of livestock – county analysis (3-year period)
- area under crops and pasture
- number of livestock
- area farmed, distinguishing area under crops, pasture and rough grazing in each

province and county
- number of cattle in each province and county
- number of sheep, horses, goats and farmed deer in each province and county
- number of pigs and poultry in each region

Estimated area, yield and production of crops

Estimated output, input and income in agriculture
- output of cattle and calves, pigs, sheep and lambs, milk output and disposal, farm produce and fuel consumed in farm households.

Monthly pig slaughterings at licensed bacon factories

Meat supply balance figures
- data for total meat, beef and veal, pig meat, sheep meat, poultry meat.

Agricultural labour input
- number of farms classified by farm size
- number of family farms classified by characteristics of holder
- family and regular non-family workers: number of persons classified by age and annual work units
- family and regular non-family workers: number of persons classified by sex and category of worker
- total labour input: number of annual work units classified by category of worker

Forestry operations
- acquisition of land by Coillte Teoranta for planting purposes, number of persons permanently employed and amounts of wages paid

Agricultural land sales
- average agricultural land transaction size each quarter
- average price per hectare of agricultural land
- average price per acre of agricultural land
- number of agricultural land transactions each quarter
- average agricultural land transaction size by region

Milk output and disposal

Cereals supply
- principal crops, seeds, feeding stuffs, industrial uses.

Central Statistics Office
STATISTICAL RELEASES
Dublin: Central Statistics Office

Statistical Releases issued by the Central Statistics Office update the information and statistics in the *Statistical Bulletin*. Listed below are the *Releases* issued for agriculture.

- Estimated output, input and income in agriculture (annual)
  – Advance (annual)
  – Preliminary (annual)

- – Final (annual)
- June survey – provisional estimates (annual)
- June survey – final estimates (annual)
- Livestock survey – December (annual)
- Pig survey – April (annual)
- Pig survey – August (annual)
- Distribution of cattle and pigs by size of herd (biennial)
- Pig slaughterings (annual)
- Meat supply balance (annual)
- Estimated area, yield and production of crops (annual)
- Agricultural labour input (annual)
- Production of milk and milk products (weekly)

Agriculture Statistics – historical series
This is a special release. It provides a historical review for the period 1847 to 1996 for the following items:
- area under the principal crops (wheat, oats, barley, potatoes, turnips, sugarbeet)
- number of livestock (cattle, cows, sheep, ewes, pigs, poultry, horses and ponies)
- number of agricultural holdings classified by size
- total population counts classified by county.

Department of Agriculture, Food and Forestry*
ANNUAL REPORT OF THE MINISTER FOR AGRICULTURE, FOOD AND FORESTRY
Dublin: Stationery Office (annually)

The *Annual Report* is presented to each House of the Oireachtas by the Minister for Agriculture and Food pursuant to Section 46 of the Agriculture Act, 1931. The Report is set out in the sections listed below:

A general review of the agriculture sector by the Minister for Agriculture and Food

Organisation of the Department of Agriculture and Food

Agricultural output, input and expenditure

Livestock enumeration

Farm income

European Union and international developments
- EU structural funds, price proposals, agri-monetary rules, etc.

Livestock (including poultry) and livestock products – sector analysis
- *cattle and beef* – market situation, cattle slaughterings, live cattle exports, beef exports, export refunds
- *milk and dairy products* – market situation, creamery milk prices, intervention stocks, promotion measures for milk products, hygiene standards in milk and milk products, milk market support schemes
- *sheep and wool* – market situation, production and trade
- *pigs and pigmeat* – market situation, production and trade
- *poultry and eggs* – market situation, production and trade

4

Forestry
- CAP Reform Afforestation Programme 1993–1997
- Operational Programme for Agriculture, Rural Development and Forestry
- strategy for the forestry sector

Arable crops, horticulture, feeding stuffs and fertilisers
- cereals and oilseed rape – production and Market Support System for Producers of Arable Crops
- potatoes – production, Seed Potato Certification Scheme, Potato Variety Evaluation Programme
- sugar beet – production and market situation
- horticulture – production, quality standards and certification
- feedingstuffs
- fertilisers

Animal production and products
- livestock headage and premiums schemes
- farm improvement schemes
- cattle improvement schemes
- livestock marts
- sheep and wool
- poultry and eggs
- horses

Crops and horticulture
- grass seed – Grass Seed Certification Scheme
- cereal seeds – Seed Certification Service
- fertilisers and lime
- plant health and pesticides

Rural development and organic farming

* Since July 1997 Department of Agriculture and Food.

Department of Agriculture, Food and Forestry*

ANNUAL REVIEW AND OUTLOOK FOR AGRICULTURE, THE FOOD INDUSTRY AND FORESTRY

Dublin: Department of Agriculture, Food and Forestry (annually)

The *Annual Review and Outlook* provides an outline of developments in the agricultural sector and highlights the chances likely to affect the sector in the short and medium terms. The *Annual Review 1995* is set out in the following sections.

The national and agricultural economy
- agricultural output and income
- interest paid and earned by farmers
- farm household income
- employment in agriculture
- agriculture in the national economy
- agricultural and food exports and imports

European Union and international developments
- GATT (General Agreement on Tariffs and Trade)
- relations with Central and Eastern Europe
- agri-monetary system
- farm prices

Agriculture structures and rural development
- Operational Programme for Agriculture, Rural Development and Forestry
- farm improvement schemes
- research, advisory services and training

Community initiatives
- LEADER Programme

Food industry
- Operational Programme for the Food Industry

Forestry
- strategy for the forestry sector
- forestry development
- reafforestation schemes

Animal health and plant health

Review of commodities
- cattle and beef, milk and milk products, poultry and eggs, sheep and lambs, pigs, cereals, root crops, etc.

Horticulture
- Outlook for agriculture and the national economy

* Since July 1997 Department of Agriculture and Food.

Department of Agriculture, Food and Forestry*
SCHEMES AND SERVICES
Dublin: Department of Agriculture, Food and Forestry (annually)

This booklet describes the various services available to the farmer and the various schemes in operation. It is set out in the sections summarised below:

- Charter of Rights for Farmers
- Structural Funds
- grants for farm improvements
- grants for livestock
- FEOGA Grants Scheme
- livestock and livestock products
- cattle (milk recording, artificial insemination, control of bulls for breeding, market support measures)
- sheep (breed improvement, Sheepmeat Producer Group Scheme)
- pigs (pig carcass grading, Pigmeat Producer Group Scheme)
- meat hygiene

- poultry and eggs
- horses and greyhounds
- feedingstuff controls
- crops and horticulture
- plant health and pesticides
- fertilisers
- rural development
- forestry
- State bodies – Teagasc, An Bord Glas, An Bord Bia.

* Since July 1997 Department of Agriculture and Food.

Department of Finance
ECONOMIC REVIEW AND OUTLOOK
Dublin: Stationery Office (annually)

The appendix in the *Economic Review and Outlook* comprises statistical tables with comparative figures for approximately nine years. The table relevant to agriculture is:

- Agricultural output, input, product and income.

Department of Foreign Affairs
DEVELOPMENTS IN THE EUROPEAN UNION
Dublin: Stationery Office (biannually)

In accordance with Section 5 of the 1972 European Communities Act, the Government is required to submit twice yearly to each House of the Oireachtas a report on the developments in the European Communities. Topics relevant to fisheries and forestry are:

- Common Fisheries Policy (CFP)
- EU Directives and Regulations
- fisheries surveillance
- fish conservation measures
- fish quotas, total allowable catches (TACs), catch declarations
- Irish fishing industry
- fish conservation measures
- protection of shellfish waters
- Operational Programme for Forestry in Ireland
- investment in Irish forestry.

Government Information Services
PRESS RELEASE issued on behalf of the Department of Agriculture and Food
Dublin: Government Information Services (fortnightly)

Information in the *Press Release* is obtained from the Department of Agriculture and Food, and coverage includes:

- announcements by the Minister for Agriculture and Food
- EU compensation for the beef sector
- milk quotas

- BSE Eradication Scheme
- investment in the food sector
- current developments in the agri-business sector
- taxation of farmers
- Stock Relief Scheme
- EU aid packages.

Other Publications: Irish

Agricultural Economics Society of Ireland
PROCEEDINGS
Dublin: Agricultural Economics Society of Ireland (annually)

Topics covered in the lectures delivered at meetings and at the Annual General Conference of the Agricultural Economics Society of Ireland include: CAP reform, the food industry and jobs, market prospects for milk products, export marketing for the Irish beef sector, performance and funding of the Irish Dairy Co-operatives, support measures necessary to retain the maximum number of milk suppliers, marketing pigmeat products in Ireland, the agricultural structures policy in the European Union, trends in food retailing in Britain and Ireland.

Bord Bia – Irish Food Board
MARKET MONITOR
Dublin: Bord Bia (weekly)

The *Market Monitor* contains up-to-date information on various issues, including:

- market situation – cattle, sheep, lambs, pigs
- cattle and beef trade
- cattle prices
- Irish cattle prices
- EU calf prices
- trends in domestic retail meat prices (cattle, lamb, pork)
- beef export refunds
- trade – cattle, sheep, lamb, pigs
- EU reference and representative prices (beef, pigmeat, sheepmeat)
- pig prices in selected EU countries
- exports of live cattle, sheep and pigs
- cattle cull update in respect of BSE
- slaughterings at meat plants
- EU Calf Schemes update
- lamb trade.

Each issue of the *Market Monitor* also contains:

- market exchange rates
- agricultural conversion rates.

An Bord Iascaigh Mhara (BIM) – the Irish Sea Fisheries Board
ANNUAL REPORT AND ACCOUNTS
Dublin: An Bord Iascaigh Mhara (annually)

An Bord Iascaigh Mhara is the State agency for the development of the seafish industry. The Chairman's Statement comments on:

- performance of the seafish industry
- fish catches
- exports of fish and fish products
- investments in the fishing fleet and in new projects
- EU grants
- performance of the fish processing plants.

The principal operating divisions of An Bord Iascaigh Mhara are:

- Sea Fisheries
- Fish Processing and Marketing
- Aquaculture
- Fleet Management and Investment in Fishing Vessels.

Coillte Teoranta – Irish Forestry Board
ANNUAL REPORT AND ACCOUNTS
Dublin: Coillte Teoranta (annually)

Coillte Teoranta was established in 1989 to manage the public forests and to develop the Irish forest industry. The Chairman's Statement and the Chief Executive's Report give a review of:

- growth and development in the Irish forestry industry and forest-related enterprises
- expansion and development of the timber processing sector
- afforestation of various areas
- supplies and sales of logs to sawmills
- participation of Coillte in overseas projects
- developments in the Irish wood-processing sector
- timber production, sales and marketing
- performance of Coillte Teo.

Irish Dairy Board Co-operative Limited
ANNUAL REPORT
Dublin: Irish Dairy Board (annually)

The Irish Dairy Board is the marketing body of its members. It is the biggest exporter of Irish dairy products and is a major food distribution company in the overseas markets. It also owns the internationally established Kerrygold brand. It was formed in 1961 as Bord Bainne Co-operative.

The *Annual Report* gives information on the following:

- principal activities of the Irish Dairy Board
- retail business
- food ingredients and products
- commodity trading.

The Chairman's Statement and the Managing Director's Report comment on:

- performance of the Irish Dairy Board
- effects of the Uruguay Round
- market conditions for dairy products in Ireland and abroad
- world dairy markets
- EU dairy market
- milk, butter and cheese production and prices
- milk supply and utilisation
- EU intervention prices.

The *Annual Report* also includes the Financial Statements and organisation and structure of the Board.

Other Publications of the Irish Dairy Board

Dairy News (monthly)
Irish Dairy Board – Facts and Figures (quarterly)

Irish Timber Growers Association
IRISH TIMBER GROWERS ASSOCIATION YEARBOOK
Kinnetty, Co. Offaly: Irish Timber Growers Association (annually)

The *Yearbook* gives a review of:

- the Irish forestry industry
- forest establishment and management
- production of timber
- imports/exports of timber
- EU forest structures (wooded areas by type of ownership)
- Afforestation Grant Scheme: levels of aid.

National Milk Agency
ANNUAL REPORT AND ACCOUNTS
Dublin: National Milk Agency (annually)

The National Milk Agency was established on 30 December 1994. Its principal function is to regulate the supply of milk for liquid consumption throughout the State in accordance with the provisions of the Milk (Regulation of Supply) Act, 1994.

The Statements of the Chairman and Chief Executive have information on:

- achievements and operations of the Agency
- the liquid milk industry
- the liquid milk market
- national milk supplies
- milk imports for liquid milk consumption
- milk price trends
- types of registered contracts
- payment systems for liquid milk.

Teagasc – the Agriculture and Food Development Authority
ANNUAL REPORT AND ACCOUNTS
Dublin: Teagasc (annually)

Teagasc is the national body providing advisory, research, education and training services to the agriculture and food industry. It was established in September 1988 under the Agriculture (Research, Training and Advice) Act, 1988. It replaced ACOT, the agricultural advisory and training body and An Foras Taluntais, the agriculture and food research organisation.

The *Annual Report* contains information on:

- the role, organisation and structure of Teagasc
- services provided by Teagasc
- agri-food economic research programme
- rural development research programme
- dairy production research programme
- milk production and milk schemes
- beef research programme
- beef production systems
- sheep production systems
- pig production systems
- crops research programme
- production of cereals, potatoes, sugarbeet, etc.
- horticulture and vegetable production
- Teagasc publications.

Teagasc – the Agriculture and Food Development Authority
IRISH AGRICULTURE IN FIGURES
Dublin: Teagasc (annually)

This booklet comprises statistical tables including:

- population and labour force
- number of farms by size of farm
- land use
- agricultural output
- inputs of materials and services
- output and income in agriculture
- livestock numbers – June
- direct income payments and levies in agriculture
- agriculture and food exports
- milk output, disposal and exports
- output of cattle, pigs, sheep and lambs
- trend in certain price indices
- per capita consumption of foodstuffs
- production of compound feedingstuffs
- fertiliser consumption
- employment in food and other industrial sectors
- farm equipment and machinery
- output, expenses and income by size of farm and by system of farming
- agriculture in the European Union

- livestock numbers in the EU
- meat consumption in the EU
- application of milk quota system in the EU.

Teagasc – the Agriculture and Food Development Authority
NATIONAL FARM SURVEY
Dublin: Teagasc (annually)

The National Farm Survey is designed to determine the financial situation of Irish farms by measuring the level of gross output, costs, income, investment and indebtedness across the spectrum of farming systems and sizes.

The *National Farm Survey 1996* was published in 1997. A summary of significant events and developments in the farming sector precedes the detailed tables. The tables include:

- family farm income by system and farm size
- distribution of family farm income
- direct payments as a percentage of family farm income
- gross margins
- average new investment per farm
- farm financial results by size
- gross output and direct payments by size
- resources per farm
- farm financial results by system of farming
- resources per farm by economic size
- farm profile by region
- gross output and direct payments by system of farming.

Other Publications: British

Agra Europe (London) Ltd
AGRA EUROPE
Tunbridge Wells: Agra Europe (London) Ltd (weekly)

Agra Europe is international in scope and comprises four principal sections.

Panorama from Brussels
Current topics of significance and interest are reviewed in this section, e.g. Common Agricultural Policy (CAP) reform; milk quotas; EU cereal production; world grain market; market outlook for beef, pigmeat, eggs and poultry; olive oil production; cereals and oilseeds; dairy output; outlook for fruit and vegetables; multilateral trade agreements; EU subsidies and levies; agri-monetary forecasts; Green Rate devaluations; and support price changes.

Markets
Text and statistical tables for agricultural commodities, livestock, cereals and potatoes as regards prices, production, consumption, marketing and imports/exports are contained in this section.

European Union
Agricultural developments and policies within the EU and EU trade agreement with non-EU countries.

National

The agricultural situation; significant agricultural news and developments in selected countries.

Meat and Livestock Commission (MLC)

EUROPEAN MARKET SURVEY: a weekly report on the international meat market

Milton Keynes: Meat and Livestock Commission (weekly)

The *European Market Survey* covers topics such as German beef production, EU inflation rate, EU stocks of intervention beef, sheep numbers in selected EU countries, pig numbers in France and Austria, changes in the Green Rate, Calf Scheme update, French imports of live sheep, illegal exports of UK beef, applications for export licences for exporting live animals, frozen/fresh/chilled beef.

The tables in each issue give figures for:

- beef and veal import tariffs
- beef and veal export refunds
- pigmeat refunds and tariffs
- conversion rates – the EU and other currencies
- finished cattle and calf prices – all EU countries (with % change on previous week and previous year)
- finished pig prices – all EU countries (% change on previous week and year)
- Dutch pig futures
- reference prices in ECUs for beef, pigmeat, sheepmeat (with % change on previous week and year)
- finished lamb prices – EU lamb-producing countries.

The *European Market Survey* also contains the *Official Journal* news, i.e. the latest Regulations and Decisions of the Commission of the European Union.

Meat and Livestock Commission (MLC)

INTERNATIONAL MEAT MARKET REVIEW

Milton Keynes: Meat and Livestock Commission (biannually)

The *International Meat Market Review* gives a global review of the meat market and a review of the principal meat-producing countries.

World review

Beef, sheepmeat, poultry: situation and outlook

Country reviews

Cattle sector (live cattle exports, cattle prices, slaughterings, beef production, veal production, beef exports, exports/imports, demand and consumption, cattle outlook)

Sheep sector (sheep breeding, sheep and lamb slaughterings, exports of sheepmeat, prices, sheepmeat production, demand and consumption, sheepmeat outlook)

Pig sector (breeding herds, number of pigs, live pig exports, slaughterings, production of pigmeat, exports/imports of pigmeat, pork prices, demand and consumption, pig outlook

---

ECONOMIC INFORMATION: IRELAND

Meat and Livestock Commission (MLC)
MEAT DEMAND TRENDS
Milton Keynes: Meat and Livestock Commission (quarterly)

Meat Demand Trends comprises text, graphs and tables. Topics covered include understanding of meat demand; consumer attitudes; the EU market; meat consumption; the market for frozen meat and meat products; who spends what in the EU; retail meat sales a year after BSE; UK bacon market; processed meat consumption in Europe; changes in EU meat consumption; meat expenditure in the EU; demand for meat in Japan, the United States and EFTA countries.

A quarterly statistical update gives:

- key UK economic indicators update
- expenditure and consumption update
- prices update.

National Dairy Council
DAIRY FACTS AND FIGURES
London: National Dairy Council (annually)

The 1996 edition of *Dairy Facts and Figures* was published in 1997. It mainly covers the United Kingdom, but also has a section on the European Union. Figures are given for each EU Member Country in the following tables:

- land, area, population and employment
- unemployment, GDP, inflation, consumer food expenditure
- shares of individual products in final agricultural production
- cattle population
- dairy cow numbers
- distribution of dairy herds by herd size
- milk yields
- cow's milk delivered to dairies relative to quota – percentage
- producer milk prices in national currency
- sales of liquid milk by dairies to the domestic market
- butter production
- cheese production
- condensed and evaporated milk production
- whole milk powder production
- skimmed milk production.

Publications: International Organisations

European Communities, Commission
THE AGRICULTURAL SITUATION IN THE COMMUNITY (published in conjunction with the General Report on the Activities of the European Union)
Luxembourg: Office for Official Publications of the European Communities (annually)

This report provides a detailed review of agricultural developments within the Community. Text and tables give information and figures for:

- current developments in the agricultural situation in the EU Member States and Central and

Eastern European countries
- CAP reform
- agricultural production and price trends
- trends in farm incomes
- general domestic situation
- international trade agreements, such as the Uruguay Round
- markets for cereals, rice, sugar, olive oil, fruit, vegetables, wine, tobacco, animal feedingstuffs, milk and milk products, beef and veal, sheepmeat, poultrymeat, eggs, potatoes, etc.
- agricultural markets for agricultural products
- consumption and self-sufficiency
- agricultural economy – basic statistics
- agricultural production and consumption
- prices and production costs
- EU price indices for feedingstuffs and fertilisers
- financial aspects: expenditure on the Common Agricultural Policy (CAP), EAGGF Guarantee and Guidance expenditure by Member State
- trend of purchase prices of agricultural inputs
- producer prices in EU Member States
- employment in agriculture (breakdown by type of labour, numbers employed, working hours, etc.)
- land use (main crops, area used for the principal agricultural products, livestock numbers)
- farm structures (number and area of holdings)
- trade (imports/exports, EU share of the world market, EU trade by product, intra- and inter-EU trade).

European Communities, Eurostat (Statistical Office of the EC)
AGRICULTURAL INCOME
Luxembourg: Office for Official Publications of the European Communities (annually)

The *Agricultural Income 1995* report, published in 1996, comments on:

- changes in agricultural income in the EU in 1995 over 1994
  – main results: an overview
  – final agricultural output
  – crop output
  – animal output
  – indicators of agricultural income in the EU
- changes in agricultural income in the Member States in 1995 over 1994
- long-term trends in agricultural income in the EU from 1980 to 1995
- long-term trends in agricultural income in the Member States from 1980 to 1995
- comparison of agricultural income levels in the Member States of the EU
- total income of agricultural households.

European Communities, Eurostat (Statistical Office of the EC)
AGRICULTURE – STATISTICAL YEARBOOK
Luxembourg: Office for Official Publications of the European Communities (annually)

Agriculture – Statistical Yearbook covers agriculture, forestry and fisheries. Detailed tables contain figures for the following.

Land use, animal production, crop production
- selected crop production in the world
- livestock numbers in the world and in the EU
- meat production in the world and in the EU
- total agricultural area and land use
- employment by sector of activity
- gross value added at factor cost by group of economic branches
- EU trade in agricultural commodities, food and live animals
- crop production
- supply balance sheets of crops, fruit and vegetables
- animal production (cows, pigs, sheep, goats)
- production of eggs and milk
- land use

Structure of agricultural holdings
- agricultural holdings by area, by size classes and utilisation
- holdings by type of farming
- total labour force
- labour force by farm type
- managers by age classes
- holdings by breeding stock

Price and price indices
- selling prices of crop products and animal products
- purchase prices of the means of agricultural production
- EU index of producer prices of agricultural products
- EU index of purchase prices of the means of agricultural production
- consumer price index for food

Agricultural accounts
- individual EU Member States' shares in the value of output in the EU
- main items of final output and intermediate consumption
- indices of net income of total agricultural labour
- indices of net income of agricultural family labour (ten-year period)

Forestry
- forest and other wooded area as percentage of total area
- agricultural holdings with wooded area
- roundwood production
- supply balance sheet for roundwood

Fisheries
- total catch of fish
- catch by fishing region
- catch by main species
- fishing fleet (numbers and tonnage).

European Communities, Eurostat (Statistical Office of the EC)
ANIMAL PRODUCTION – QUARTERLY STATISTICS
Luxembourg: Office for Official Publications of the European Communities (quarterly)

The *Animal Production – Quarterly Statistics* bulletin comprises tables which contain:
- monthly statistics on meat
  - net production (slaughterings)
  - imports of live animals
  - exports of live animals
- monthly statistics on eggs and poultry
  - chicks placed
  - utilisation of hatcheries (incubations and hatchings)
  - external trade in chicks
- monthly and annual statistics on milk and milk products
  - collection of cow's milk
  - milk products obtained
  - stocks of skimmed milk powder and butter
  - dairies – activities
- supply balance sheets.

European Communities, Eurostat (Statistical Office of the EC)
CROP PRODUCTION – Half-Yearly Statistics
Luxembourg: Office for Official Publications of the European Communities (biannually)

The *Crop Production* bulletin comprises statistical tables which contain figures for:
- land use
  - main crops area
  - land area
  - wooded area
  - utilised agricultural area
  - water supply
- crop products
  - harvested area and production (wheat, barley, rye, cereals)
- vegetables
  - harvested area and production
- fruits
  - production statistics
- supply balance sheets
  - oilseeds and fruits, oilcakes, fats and oils.

European Communities, Eurostat (Statistical Office of the EC)
ECONOMIC ACCOUNTS FOR AGRICULTURE AND FORESTRY
Luxembourg: Office for Official Publications of the European Communities (annually)

Explanatory notes and conversion rates in ECUs (European currency units) and PPS (purchasing power standard) accompany the detailed statistical tables. Examples include:

- agricultural accounts (national level)
- comparative tables
  - final agricultural output
  - final crop output
  - final animal output
  - consumption (volume indices and price indices)
  - gross value added at market prices

- subsidies
- net operating surplus
- net income from all agricultural activity
- gross fixed capital formation
- forestry accounts (national level)
- agricultural accounts (regional level).

European Communities, Eurostat (Statistical Office of the EC)
FISHERIES – YEARLY STATISTICS
Luxembourg: Office for Official Publications of the European Communities (annually)

Explanatory notes and conversion tables accompany the statistical tables, which contain figures for:

- catches by major fishing region
- catches of principal species of fish
- Eurostat Register of Fishing Fleets (numbers, tonnage, length and power of vessels)
- foreign trade in fish and fish products (value and quantity).

European Communities, Eurostat (Statistical Office of the EC)
STATISTICS IN FOCUS – Agriculture, Forestry and Fisheries
Luxembourg: Office for Official Publications of the European Communities (several issues per annum)

Statistics in Focus is a brief bulletin which summarises the main results of surveys, studies or publications undertaken by Eurostat. Topics covered include:

- surveys on the number of cattle, pigs, sheep and goats carried out in the European Union in December 1995
- developments in the volume of agricultural labour input in the European Union
- total income of agricultural households: 1995 report
- trends in the EU agricultural price indices (input and output)
- agriculture in the three newest Member States – Austria, Finland, Sweden
- results of the August 1996 survey of the pig population
- results of the May–June 1996 cattle population survey.

European Communities, Eurostat (Statistical Office of the EC)
TOTAL INCOME OF AGRICULTURAL HOUSEHOLDS
Luxembourg: Office for Official Publications of the European Communities (annually)

The *Total Income of Agricultural Households 1995* report was published in 1996. The text is supported by tables, graphs and charts. The report is divided into two parts:

Part 1: General report
Part 2: Country reports

For Ireland the main source of data on disposable income of households is the *Household Budget Survey*.

Food and Agricultural Organization (FAO)
FAO QUARTERLY BULLETIN OF STATISTICS
Rome: FAO (quarterly)

The *FAO Quarterly Bulletin of Statistics* is international in scope and provides the most up-to-date statistics on agricultural production. Explanatory notes precede the tables, which contain figures for:

- agricultural production (crops, cereals, fruit, vegetables, tea, wine, tobacco, etc.)
- livestock numbers (cattle, pigs, chickens, horses, etc.).

Food and Agriculture Organization (FAO)
FERTILIZER YEARBOOK
Rome: FAO (annually)

The *Fertilizer Yearbook* is international in scope. Explanatory notes, exchange rates, a list of countries, and a list of products precede the statistical tables. Examples include:

- world production, consumption, trade and supply of fertilisers
- nitrogeneous fertilisers, phosphate and potash – production, trade and consumption by economic class (i.e. developed market economies and developing market economies)
- estimated production of potash
- potash exports in the form of complex fertilisers
- consumption indicators of lime
- consumption of fertilisers per hectare of agricultural area, arable land and permanent crops
- production of ammonia
- imports/exports of phosphate, potash and nitrogeneous fertilisers
- prices and subsidies: index numbers of prices received by farmers and prices paid by farmers for farming requisites, and fertiliser subsidies.

Food and Agriculture Organization (FAO)
FISHERY STATISTICS: Catches and Landings
Rome: FAO (annually)

Explanatory notes and currency codes precede the detailed statistical tables summarised below:

- world summary
  - world catches by species groupings; by country; catches in inland waters and in sea water
  - production of seaweeds and other aquatic plants by country
- catches by species groups (species have been grouped according to the *International Standard Statistical Classification of Aquatic Animals and Plants*)
- catches by major fishing areas and species groups
- catches by continent.

Food and Agriculture Organization (FAO)
FISHERY STATISTICS: Commodities
Rome: FAO (annually)

Explanatory notes, exchange rates and symbols precede the detailed statistical tables arranged in sections summarised below:

- world catches (ten-year period)
- estimated total international trade in fishery commodities
- international trade in fishery commodities by principal importers and exporters
- total of seven fishery commodity groups, by continent, country or area
- imports and exports by country and by seven fishery commodity groups
- selected fishery commodities: production, imports, exports by country or area
- consumption of fishery products
- world catches: estimated landed value by groups of species.

Food and Agriculture Organization (FAO)
PRODUCTION YEARBOOK
Rome: FAO (annually)

Explanatory notes precede the tables which are divided into sections including:

- land
  – total area, arable land, land under permanent crops, pastures and forests
- population
  – total population and agricultural population
- FAO indices of agricultural production
  – total food production
  – total agricultural production
  – total crop production
  – total production of livestock products
  – total cereal production
  – per capita production
- statistical summary
  – a statistical summary of world and continental agricultural production
- crops
  – cereals, vegetables, fruits, industrial crops, oilseeds, nuts, wine, etc.
- livestock numbers and products
  – livestock numbers
  – slaughterings and production of meat
  – milk, cheese and livestock products
- means of production
  – farm machinery.

Food and Agriculture Organization (FAO)
THE STATE OF FOOD AND AGRICULTURE
Rome: FAO (annually)

The State of Food and Agriculture gives:

- a review of the world agricultural situation
- crop and livestock production
- cereal supplies, stocks and utilisation
- international agricultural prices

- fisheries: fish catches and trade
- forestry: timber production and trade
- performance of the agricultural sector
- agricultural subsidies and food prices
- the agricultural situation in various countries.

Food and Agriculture Organization (FAO)/United Nations.Economic Commission for Europe (ECE)
TIMBER BULLETIN
Geneva: United Nations (quarterly)

Each issue of the *Timber Bulletin* deals with a specific topic, such as:

- forest products prices
- forest products statistics
- forest products annual market review
- forest fire statistics
- forest products markets in 1996 and prospects for 1997.

Food and Agriculture Organization (FAO)/United Nations. Economic Commission for Europe (ECE)
TIMBER BULLETIN – FOREST PRODUCTS ANNUAL MARKET REVIEW
Geneva: United Nations (quarterly)

Forest Products Annual Market Review 1996–1997, published in 1997, comprises text, charts, graphs and tables. It gives:

- an overview of forest products markets
- economic situation of Europe, Russian Federation and North America
- developments for construction
- furniture market
- trends in supply, trade and consumption of forest products
- consumption of roundwood, coniferous sawnwood, sawn hardwood, plywood, hardboard, etc.

Food and Agriculture Organization (FAO)/United Nations. Economic Commission for Europe (ECE)
TIMBER BULLETIN – FOREST PRODUCTS STATISTICS
Geneva: United Nations (quarterly)

Forest Products Statistics 1992–1996, published in 1997, provides statistical information on forest products in the UN–ECE region of Europe, North America, the Russian Federation and Japan.
    The tables contain figures for production, imports and exports of fuelwood, industrial round-wood, pulpwood, logs, sawnwood, wood panels, woodpulp, paper and paperboard, etc.

Organisation for Economic Co-operation and Development (OECD)
AGRICULTURAL OUTLOOK
Paris: OECD (annually)

Agricultural Outlook 1997–2001 is the third edition of this publication and provides a five-year assessment of future trends and prospects in the major agricultural commodity markets. It also assesses the impact of policy changes and global economic developments on international prices and trade.

The text is accompanied by charts, graphs and tables. Each report gives:

- an overview of the agricultural markets
- agricultural policies and developments in OECD countries
- economic growth and performance of the agricultural sector
- trade agreements
- principal developments in:
  – *cereals* (current situation; production; prices; trade; global grain stocks; outlook for cereals, coarse grains and wheat)
  – *oilseeds* (current situation; production; consumption; supplies; world oilseed prices; trade in oilseeds and oilseed products; outlook for the oilseed market)
  – *meat* (current situation; production; demand; consumption of beef; pigmeat/pork; poultry; price outlook; developments in the world meat markets; EU's beef policy; the meat trade; effect of the BSE outbreak on the beef market; outlook for the meat market)
  – *milk and dairy products* (current situation; production and consumption of milk and milk powder; prices for butter and skim milk powder; dairy quotas in OECD countries; dairy prices; trade; production of butter and cheese; outlook for dairy products)
  – *sugar* (current market situation; production; consumption; world raw sugar prices; world demand; trade; sugar policy; outlook for the sugar market)
- statistical tables
  – projections for cereals, coarse grains, oilseeds, oilseed oil, meat, pigmeat, pork, beef and veal, poultrymeat, sheepmeat, milk, butter, cheese, sugar, whole and skim milk powder.

Organisation for Economic Co-operation and Development (OECD)
AGRICULTURAL POLICIES IN OECD COUNTRIES
Paris: OECD (annually)

Agricultural Policies in OECD Countries 1997 is the tenth report in this series. These reports comprise text, graphs and tables, and cover topics such as:

- agricultural policy developments in OECD countries
- the World Trade Organization and trade agreements
- trade dispute developments involving agricultural products
- agricultural trade situation
- markets and trade: situation and outlook for major commodities
- assistance to agriculture
- reform of agricultural policies.

Tables contain figures for:

- OECD cereal market, oilseed market, meat market, dairy market
- European Union: agricultural income, producer subsidies, consumer subsidies
- key agricultural indicators
- regional trade flows for selected agricultural products
- change in OECD trade volumes
- change in world commodity prices
- change in world trade volumes.

Organisation for Economic Co-operation and Development (OECD)
MEAT BALANCES IN OECD COUNTRIES
Paris: OECD (annually)

Definitions, explanatory notes, sources of data used and methodology employed precede the tables, which are divided into two parts:

General tables
- population statistics
- livestock numbers (cattle, pigs, sheep)
- meat production (total meat, beef and veal, pigmeat, poultrymeat, mutton, lamb, goatmeat, horsemeat, edible offals, etc.)
- foreign trade
- total meat consumption and consumption per head

Country tables
- number of animals slaughtered
- meat production (beef, veal, pigmeat, sheepmeat, lamb, goatmeat, horsemeat, poultrymeat)
- exports of live animals
- exports/imports of meat
- stock variations
- net trade balance

Organisation for Economic Co-operation and Development (OECD)
REVIEW OF FISHERIES IN OECD MEMBER COUNTRIES
Paris: OECD (annually)

The *Review of Fisheries in OECD Member Countries* comprises three parts.

General survey
This survey gives an overall review of the fishing industry, information on international fishing agreements, total available catches (TACs), fish catches, aquaculture, fish consumption, international trade in fresh and frozen fish, situation in stocks of various species, OECD fishing fleets and number of fishermen, fish production, OECD imports/exports of fish by major product groups.

Country reports
For each OECD member country an appraisal is given of the fishing industry, Government policies, fish catches and landings, total allowable catches (TACs), national landings, employment in fishing, fish production, processing and marketing, exports/imports of fish and fish products, aquaculture, fish quotas, number of registered fishing vessels, outlook for the fishing industry.

Statistical annexe

United Nations. Department for Economic and Social Information and Policy Analysis
STATISTICAL YEARBOOK
New York: United Nations (annually)

The *Statistical Yearbook* is international in scope. Countries are listed in alphabetical order. Figures for agriculture, forestry and fishing are contained in a table encaptioned

'Agricultural production index numbers (cereals; oil crops; livestock; roundwood; fish catches; fertilisers)'.

United States. Department of Agriculture. Economic Research Service
AGRICULTURAL OUTLOOK
Washington, D.C.: Department of Agriculture (monthly)

This bulletin gives a global review of:

- main developments in the major markets
- global agricultural situation
- performance of various markets
- production of grain, tobacco, various cereals, potatoes, etc.
- overview of livestock, poultry and crops
- world agricultural trade
- commodity prices
- outlook for various commodities
- outlook for beef, pork, poultry and frozen products.

Balance of Payments

Central Statistics Office
ECONOMIC SERIES
Dublin: Stationery Office (monthly)

The *Economic Series* bulletin provides up-to-date information and five years' retrospection for a selection of 151 principal short-term economic series. Longer retrospection is given in each December issue. Charts and graphs accompany the tables. The numbers pertaining to the balance of payments are:

8.01	Merchandise balance
8.02	Services
8.03	Factor income
8.04	Transfers
8.05	Total current account balance.

Central Statistics Office
NATIONAL INCOME AND EXPENDITURE
Dublin: Stationery Office (annually)

Tables relevant to balance of international payments are given. Figures are given for a 7-year period in the tables summarised below.

Table – Balance of International Payments: current account

- merchandise
- international freight
- other transportation
- tourism and travel
- royalties, licences, etc.
- remuneration of employees
- investment income
- reinvested earnings
- current transfers

Table – Balance of International Payments: capital and financial account and net residual

- capital transfers (private and semi-State companies)
- official capital (Exchequer foreign borrowing)
- transactions of credit institutions
- official external reserves
- net balance on capital and financial account

Central Statistics Office
STATISTICAL ABSTRACT
Dublin: Stationery Office (annually)

Each issue of the *Statistical Abstract* contains a section on Balance of International Payments. The tables are supported by an explanatory text. Examples from the 1996 *Statistical Abstract* are:

- balance of international payments – current account, 1990–1995
- summary of current account balances, 1990–1995
- balance of international payments – capital and financial account and net residual, 1990–1995
- summary of capital and financial account balances and net residual, 1990–1995
- official external reserves: expressed in Irish pounds, 1990–1995.

Central Statistics Office
STATISTICAL BULLETIN + Index
Dublin: Stationery Office (quarterly)

Particulars of the balance of international payments are published in each issue. An explanatory text accompanies the tables, which give figures for:

- current account balances (merchandise, services, current transfers)
- capital and financial account balances and net residual (capital transfers, private capital, official capital, credit institutions transfers, official external reserves).

Central Statistics Office
STATISTICAL RELEASES
Dublin: Central Statistics Office

Statistical Releases issued by the Central Statistics Office update the information and statistics in the *Statistical Bulletin*. The *Release* issued for balance of international payments is:

Balance of International Payments (quarterly).

Department of Finance
ECONOMIC REVIEW AND OUTLOOK
Dublin: Stationery Office (annually)

The appendix in the *Economic Review and Outlook* comprises statistical tables with comparative figures for approximately nine years. The table relevant to balance of payments is:

'Balance of International Payments'.

Publications: International Organisations

European Communities, Eurostat (Statistical Office of the EC)
BALANCE OF PAYMENTS – Quarterly Statistics
Luxembourg: Office for Official Publications of the European Communities (quarterly)

Explanatory notes, ECU conversion rates and main national publications giving balance of payments data precede the statistical tables summarised below.

Tables by heading
- goods and services
- transportation
- government services
- investment income
- current and capital transfers
- direct investment abroad
- portfolio investment (assets/liabilities)

Country tables
- individual country tables include the EU Member States, United States and Japan.

Current account
- goods
- services (transportation, travel, Government services)
- income (earnings from work, compensation of employees, investment income)
- current transfers

Capital account

Financial account
- direct investment abroad
- portfolio investment (assets/liabilities)
- reserve assets

European Communities, Eurostat (Statistical Office of the EC)
BALANCE OF PAYMENTS OF THE COMMUNITY INSTITUTIONS
Luxembourg: Office for Official Publications of the European Communities (annually)

Balance of Payments of the Community Institutions 1994 was published in 1996. Explanatory notes and the methodology used precede the main sections summarised below.

Global situation 1994

Detailed analysis and trends
- current balances
- financial operations

Country tables

Credit
- goods and services
- interest receivable
- current transfers receivable

Debit
- merchandise
- services
- wages and salaries
- interest payable
- current and capital transfers payable

- change in credit–debit position of the institutions with each Member State
- balance of payments of the EU institutions (current account/capital and financial account)

Geographical breakdown
- transactions with Member States

Balance of payments – breakdown by institution
- current account
- capital and financial account

International Monetary Fund (IMF)
BALANCE OF PAYMENT STATISTICS YEARBOOK (Part 1 and Parts 2 and 3)
Washington, D.C.: International Monetary Fund (annually)

Part 1 – Country tables
- figures for 160 countries (eight-year period)
- current account (goods, services, current transfers: credit/debit)
- financial account (direct investment abroad and at home, portfolio investment: assets/liabilities, other investment: assets/liabilities)
- capital account (capital transfers: credit/debit)

Part 2 – World and regional tables
Figures for:

- current account balances
- capital account balances
- financial account balances
- portfolio investment
- reserve assets
- global discrepancies in balance of payments
- exports and imports of goods and services as a percentage of GDP.

Part 3 – Methodologies, compilation practices and data sources

---

United Nations. Department for Economic and Social Information and Policy Analysis
STATISTICAL YEARBOOK
New York: United Nations (annually)

The *Statistical Yearbook* is international in scope. Countries are listed in alphabetical order. Balance of payments figures are contained in the following tables:

- balance of payments (millions of US dollars)
- goods: exports/imports
- services and income (credit/debit)
- current transactions (credit)
- current transfers (debit)
- capital account (credit/debit)
- financial account
- reserves.

Consumption

Central Statistics Office
HOUSEHOLD BUDGET SURVEY
Dublin: Stationery Office (every seven years)

The large-scale national *Household Budget Surveys* cover 7,000–8,000 urban and rural households. Estimates are provided for household composition, accommodation facilities, weekly income, weekly expenditure (over 300 categories of goods and services are distinguished) and other miscellaneous items classified by various household characteristics such as size, composition, gross income level and location.

Large-scale national surveys were conducted in respect of the years 1973, 1980, 1987 and 1994–95.

Central Statistics Office
HOUSEHOLD BUDGET SURVEY 1994–95 (2 volumes)
Volume 1 – Detailed results for all households
Dublin: Stationery Office, 1997

This contains the following.

Summary results for 1994–95 and comparison with 1987

Tables (examples)
- average size, composition, household income and expenditure (maximum detail), 1994–95 classified by urban/rural location
- average size, composition, household income and expenditure (maximum detail), 1994–95 classified by:
  – gross household income
  – regional authority regions
  – household tenure
  – social group of reference person
  – livelihood status of household person
  – household size
  – household composition
- average size, composition, household income and expenditure (intermediate detail), 1994–95
- average size, composition, household income and expenditure (minimum detail), 1994–95 classified by:
  – gross household income and social group of reference person
  – gross household income and household tenure
  – gross household income and livelihood status of reference person
  – household size and household tenure
  – household size and social group of reference person
  – regional authority region and household tenure
  – regional authority region and social group of reference person
  – regional authority region and livelihood status of reference person
  – regional authority region and household size

Central Statistics Office
HOUSEHOLD BUDGET SURVEY 1994–95 (2 volumes)
Volume 2: Detailed results for urban and rural households
Dublin: Central Statistics Office, 1997

This comprises statistical tables arranged in three parts as follows:

Part 1 – Urban households
- average size, accommodation, household income and expenditure 1994–95 classified by gross household income
- average size, composition, household income and expenditure 1994–95 classified by town size, tenure, social group, livelihood status of person, household size, household composition, family cycle, gross household income and household size
- average size, composition, household income and expenditure 1994–95 classified by:
  – gross household income and town size
  – gross household income and household tenure
  – gross household income and social group of reference person
  – gross household income and livelihood status of reference person

Part 2 – Rural households
This part contains similar information to Part 1

Part 3 – Rural farm households
- average size, composition, household income and expenditure 1994–95 classified by gross household income
- average size, composition, household income and expenditure 1994–95 classified by:
  – acreage farmed
  – planning region
  – household size
  – household composition
- average size, composition, household income and expenditure 1994–95 classified by:
  – gross household income and acreage farmed
  – gross household income and household size
  – gross household income and planning region

Central Statistics Office
STATISTICAL BULLETIN + Index
Dublin: Stationery Office (quarterly)

The Retail Sales Index is published in each issue of the *Statistical Bulletin*. It measures changes in both the value and volume levels of retail sales on a seasonally adjusted basis for 14 types of retail businesses excluding garages. The methodology is given in the March 1994 issue of the *Statistical Bulletin*.

The principal tables are:

- seasonally adjusted indices of total retail sales
- seasonally adjusted value indices of retail sales for 14 retail businesses
- seasonally adjusted volume indices of retail sales for 14 retail businesses
- seasonally unadjusted value indices of retail sales for 14 retail businesses
- seasonally unadjusted volume indices of retail sales for 14 retail businesses.

Central Statistics Office
STATISTICAL RELEASES
Dublin: Central Statistics Office

Statistical Releases issued by the Central Statistics Office update the information and statistics in the *Statistical Bulletin*. The *Release* issued for distribution is:

Retail Sales Index (monthly).

Publications: International Organisations

United Nations. Department for Economic and Social Information and Policy Analysis
STATISTICAL YEARBOOK
New York: United Nations (annually)

The *Statistical Yearbook* is international in scope. Countries are listed in alphabetical order. Figures for private consumption are contained in the table encaptioned

'Private final consumption expenditure by type and purpose at current prices'.

Distribution

Central Statistics Office
ANNUAL SERVICES INQUIRY - Retail, Wholesale, Hotels, and Catering Sectors
Dublin: Stationery Office (annually)

Following the 1998 *Census of Services*, the CSO initiated a programme to update statistics on the services sectors on an annual basis. This involves annual surveys of the major retail and wholesale sectors, with most of the remaining sectors being surveyed in rotation over a three-year period. The fourth of these surveys was undertaken in 1995 and covered the 1994 trading activity of retail, wholesale, hotel, restaurant and catering enterprises. Summarised below are the tables, grouped into three main sections.

Results for the retail trade
- estimated principal aggregates for all retail enterprises in 5 retail businesses in the State
- estimated principal aggregates for all retail enterprises in 3 retail categories classified by turnover in the State
- estimated principal aggregates for all retail enterprises in 3 retail categories classified by number of persons engaged in the State

Results for the wholesale trade
- estimated principal aggregates for all wholesale enterprises in 8 wholesale businesses
- estimated principal aggregates for all wholesale enterprises in 3 wholesale categories classified by turnover in the State
- estimated principal aggregates for all wholesale enterprises in 3 wholesale categories classified by number of persons engaged in the State

Results for the hotel and catering sector
Similar tables are given for the hotel and catering sector.

Estimated supplementary aggregates accompany the principal aggregates in each section.

Central Statistics Office
CENSUS OF SERVICES
Dublin: Stationery Office (periodically)

Censuses of Distribution covering all retail and wholesale establishments were undertaken in respect of the years 1933, 1951, 1956, 1966, 1971 and 1988.

1988 Census of Services (3 volumes)
Volume 1: Detailed results for retail and wholesale trade
- *Tables* – Estimated totals for all retail outlets (number, turnover, purchases, VAT charges, gross margin, wages and salaries, persons engaged, selling space)

Volume 2: Results for non-distribution services
- *Tables* – Estimated number of outlets and persons engaged

Volume 3: Enterprise results
- *Tables* – Results for retail trade, wholesale trade, non-distribution services (estimated totals for these enterprises, number, number of trading outlets, turnover, purchases, VAT charges, stocks, gross margin, wages and salaries, persons engaged)

Central Statistics Office
ECONOMIC SERIES
Dublin: Stationery Office (monthly)

The *Economic Series* bulletin provides up-to-date information and five years' retrospection for a selection of 151 principal short-term economic series. Longer retrospection is given in each December issue.

Charts and graphs accompany the tables. The numbers pertaining to distribution are:

Retail Sales Value Index
6.01   All businesses
6.02   All businesses (SA)
6.03   All businesses excluding garages
6.04   All Businesses excluding garages (SA)

Retail Sales Volume Index
6.05   All businesses
6.06   All businesses (SA)
6.07   All businesses excluding garages
6.08   All businesses excluding garages (SA)

(SA = seasonally adjusted)

Central Statistics Office
STATISTICAL ABSTRACT
Dublin: Stationery Office (annually)

Each issue contains a section on Services and Distribution. The tables are supported by an explanatory text. Examples from the 1996 *Statistical Abstract* are as follows.

Retail enterprises
- estimated principal aggregates for all retail enterprises in 13 retail businesses in the State, 1991
- estimated principal aggregates for all retail enterprises in 5 retail businesses in the State, 1992 and 1993

Wholesale enterprises
- estimated principal aggregates for all wholesale enterprises in 8 wholesale businesses in the State, 1991, 1992, 1993
- estimated supplementary aggregates for all wholesale enterprises in 8 wholesale businesses in the State, 1991, 1992, 1993

Other enterprises
- estimated aggregates for all hotel and catering enterprises in 6 catering businesses in the State, 1991

- estimated aggregates for all business services enterprises in 7 business services in the State, 1992
- estimated aggregates for selected services enterprises in 10 services categories in the State, 1993

Retail sales
- seasonally adjusted indices of retail sales, January 1993–December 1995
- seasonally adjusted value indices of retail sales for 14 retail businesses, January 1993–December 1995
- seasonally adjusted volume indices of retail sales for 14 retail businesses, January 1993–December 1995

Central Statistics Office
STATISTICAL BULLETIN + Index
Dublin: Stationery Office (quarterly)

The Retail Sales Index is published in each issue of the *Statistical Bulletin*. It measures changes in both the value and volume levels of retail sales on a seasonally adjusted basis for 14 types of retail businesses excluding garages. The methodology is given in the March 1994 issue of the *Statistical Bulletin*.

The principal tables are:

- seasonally adjusted indices of total retail sales
- seasonally adjusted value indices of retail sales for 14 retail businesses
- seasonally adjusted volume indices of retail sales for 14 retail businesses
- seasonally unadjusted value indices of retail sales for 14 retail businesses
- seasonally unadjusted volume indices of retail sales for 14 retail businesses.

Central Statistics Office
STATISTICAL RELEASES
Dublin: Central Statistics Office

Statistical Releases issued by the Central Statistics Office update the information and statistics in the *Statistical Bulletin*. The *Release* issued for distribution is:

Retail Sales Index (monthly).

Department of Finance
ECONOMIC REVIEW AND OUTLOOK
Dublin: Stationery Office (annually)

The appendix in the *Economic Review and Outlook* comprises statistical tables with comparative figures for approximately nine years. The table relevant to distribution/retail sales is encaptioned:

'Retail sales and new private car licensing'.

Publications: International Organisations

European Communities, Eurostat (Statistical Office of the EC)
DISTRIBUTIVE TRADE AND SERVICES
Luxembourg: Office for Official Publications of the European Communities (monthly)

This monthly bulletin comprises tables which give figures for:

- distributive trade (four-year period)
  - volume of retail sales: total
  - volume of retail sales: food, beverage and tobacco
  - volume of retail sales: clothing and footwear
  - volume of retail sales: household equipment
  - first registration of private and commercial cars
- tourism (four-year period)
  - guest flows in hotels and similar establishments
  - guest flows in supplementary accommodation establishments
  - travel – balance of payments
  - passenger transport – balance of payments.

Economy: General

Official Publications

Department of Foreign Affairs
DEVELOPMENTS IN THE EUROPEAN UNION
Dublin: Stationery Office (biannually)

In accordance with Section 5 of the 1972 European Communities Act, the Government is required to submit twice yearly to each House of the Oireachtas a report on the developments in the European Communities. Topics relevant to economic policy include:

- the economic situation in the Community
- unemployment in the EU
- co-ordination of economic policies
- taxation policy
- developments in the European Monetary System (EMS)
- loans from the European Investment Bank (EIB).

Other Publications: Irish

Allied Irish Banks plc
AIB REVIEW
Dublin: Allied Irish Banks plc (quarterly)

The *AIB Review* covers topics such as:

- performance of the Irish economy
- rate of inflation
- fiscal policies
- interest rates and exchange rates
- industrial production
- retail sales
- foreign trade
- mortgage lending as percentage of personal disposable income
- national debt ratio and fiscal deficit as percentage of GNP
- Irish economic growth and prospects.

Central Bank of Ireland
ANNUAL REPORT
Dublin: Central Bank of Ireland (annually)

In addition to the Statement of Accounts, the *Annual Report* gives an appraisal of the national economy and a short-term forecast. It also has information in the following categories.

The national economy
- expenditure on Gross National Product (GNP)
- price developments
- consumer spending

- fiscal developments
- Government expenditure and revenue
- Exchequer Borrowing Requirement (EBR)
- trade and balance of payments
- industrial production
- labour market – employment, unemployment, pay

Monetary and financial market developments
- money and credit
- monetary aggregates – annual rates of change
- change in money supply
- change in private sector credit
- Irish pound exchange rates
- interest rate and bond-yield differentials
- sales of Government securities
- financing the Exchequer Borrowing Requirement (EBR)

International developments
- economic developments in the major economies such the United States, Japan, Germany, France
- developments in the major currencies – US dollar, pound sterling, Japanese yen, German mark
- European Union, Exchange Rate Mechanism (ERM)
- three-month Euro-currency interest rates

Statistical appendix
- list of reporting institutions
- list of credit institutions
- list of authorised money brokers
- investment business firms authorised by the Central Bank
- main monetary indicators
- interest rates, exchange rates, balance of payments
- banking and financial institutions – assets and liabilities
- credit institutions and building societies – balance sheets
- transactions on the Irish Pound Forward Rate Agreement Market

Public finances
- Government debt
- servicing the national debt
- Government expenditure, revenue and borrowing
- Government saving schemes
- State-sponsored bodies – assets and liabilities

Economic indicators

All issues of the Central Bank of Ireland's *Annual Report* and *Quarterly Bulletin* contain 'special articles'.

Central Bank of Ireland
IRISH ECONOMIC STATISTICS
Dublin: Central Bank of Ireland (annually)

ECONOMIC INFORMATION: IRELAND

This is a fold-out booklet published annually with the autumn issue of the *Quarterly Bulletin*. The tables contain figures for the current year, previous year and previous tenth year. Figures are given for the following:

National product
- consumers' expenditure
- public current expenditure
- fixed investment
- exports/imports of goods and services

Industrial production
- mining and quarrying
- manufacturing industries
- chemicals
- metals and engineering
- food, drink and tobacco
- textile industry
- clothing, footwear and leather
- timber and wooden furniture
- paper and printing

Building and construction
- housing stock
- public capital expenditure
- output of building and construction industry

Agriculture
- gross agricultural product
- cattle numbers
- milk output

Manpower
- total labour force
- numbers unemployed
- numbers employed in agriculture and industry
- industrial disputes (total man-days lost through industrial disputes)

Income
- national income
- weekly earnings in industry (men and women)
- weekly hours worked (men and women)

Prices
- Consumer Price Index
- Wholesale Price index
- import/export prices

External trade
- imports/exports

Balance of payments
- balance on current account

- net balance on capital and financial account
- official external reserves (end December)

Government finance
- current revenue (direct taxation, indirect taxation, non-tax revenue)
- current expenditure
- current budget deficit (surplus)
- Exchequer Borrowing Requirement
- external Government debt (end December)

Banking statistics
- currency
- narrow money supply
- wide money supply

Private sector credit
- licensed banks
- all credit institutions

Selected interest rates/yields (end year)
- Central Bank short-term facility
- Associated Banks' prime lending rate
- Interbank one-month fixed rate
- Associated Banks' deposit rate demand deposits
- building societies (investment share accounts; representative yield on Irish Government securities with five years to maturity; Equity Index)
- exchange rate (Irish pound against pound sterling, US dollar, Deutsche mark)

Indicators of living standards
- retail sales (volume)
- private motor cars
- new car registrations
- telephones and television sets

Central Bank of Ireland
MONTHLY STATISTICS
Dublin: Central Bank of Ireland (monthly)

The *Monthly Statistics* comprise tables which update the figures in the tables in the *Quarterly Bulletin* and *Annual Report* of the Central Bank.

Central Bank of Ireland
QUARTERLY BULLETIN
Dublin: Central Bank of Ireland (quarterly)

The *Quarterly Bulletin* contains information similar to that given in the *Annual Report*, e.g. the following.

The National economy
- appraisal of the national economy

- consumer spending
- investment
- fiscal developments
- trade and balance of payments
- production – industry and services
- agricultural output and incomes
- labour market – employment and unemployment

Monetary and financial market developments
- monetary policy
- money and credit
- financial markets – exchange rates and interest rates
- Irish pound exchange rates
- financing the Exchequer Borrowing Requirement (EBR)

International developments
- economic developments in the major economies
- key economic indicators

Statistical appendix – selected tables
- main economic indicators
- interest rates, exchange rates and balance of payments
- public finances
- economic indicators

All issues of the Central Bank of Ireland's *Annual Report* and *Quarterly Bulletin* contain 'special articles', such as:
- EMU and Irish monetary policy
- economic growth in Ireland: sources, potential and inflation
- inflational process in Ireland.

Economic and Social Research Institute (ESRI)
MEDIUM-TERM REVIEW
Dublin: Economic and Social Research Institute (biennially)

This gives a medium-term forecast for the Irish economy. It contains special articles as well as information on:

- performance of the Irish economy
- growth rate of Gross National Product (GNP)
- manufacturing industry – investment, output and competitiveness
- labour market – labour force, employment and unemployment
- demographic changes
- public finances
- tax reform
- National Debt and Exchequer Borrowing Requirement (EBR)
- interest rates
- balance of payments
- trade: imports/exports
- Ireland and the European Union.

Economic and Social Research Institute (ESRI)
QUARTERLY ECONOMIC COMMENTARY
Dublin: Economic and Social Research Institute (quarterly)

This contains a detailed appraisal of the domestic economy and a commentary on the international economy, US economy, UK economy, the rest of the world in the context for Ireland.

The domestic economy
- exports – goods and services
- stocks – farm stocks, Irish intervention stocks, non-agricultural stocks
- investment – gross fixed capital formation
- consumption – Government consumption and retail sales
- imports of goods and services
- balance of payments
- Gross National Product (GNP)
- agriculture – situation and outlook
- manufacturing output
- employment and unemployment
- consumer price index (CPI) – recent trend and forecast
- public finances
- interest rates

Statistical appendix

Other Publications: British

ECONOMIST, THE
London: Economist Newspaper Ltd (weekly)

In each issue of *The Economist* economic indicators are published for most European countries, Japan and the United States.

Economic indicators
- output, demand and jobs, (GDP), industrial production, retail sales (volume), unemployment (% rate)
- prices and wages (consumer prices, producer prices, wages/earnings)
- inflation rates (consumer prices, % increase on a year earlier)

Economist Intelligence Unit (EIU)
COUNTRY PROFILE
London: Economist Intelligence Unit (annually)

The EIU *Quarterly Country Report* analyses current trends and the *Annual Country Profile* provides further political and economic information. Listed below are the sections relevant to the economic situation in Ireland.

The economy
- economic structure – main economic indicators
- economic policy
- economic performance
- regional trends

Economic infrastructure
- transport and communications
- energy provision (oil, peat, hydrocarbon fuels, electricity)
- financial services
- tourism

Production
- manufacturing industry
- mining
- agriculture, forestry and fishing
- construction

The external sector
- foreign trade
- invisibles and the current account
- balance of payments
- capital flows and foreign debt
- average annual exchange rates (five-year period)

The comprehensive reference tables give figures and indices (five-year period) for:

- Government finances
- origins of Government revenue
- Public Capital Programme expenditure
- Central Government deficit as a percentage of Gross Domestic Product (GDP)
- money supply
- interest lending rates
- Gross Domestic Product (GDP) at factor cost by sector
- prices (consumer prices, wholesale prices, manufacturing output prices, agricultural output prices, import/export unit values)
- earnings (average earnings per week)
- relative wage costs in manufacturing industry
- population statistics
- structure of employment
- employment by sector in IDA-assisted companies
- employment by region in IDA-assisted companies
- Irish Stock Exchange
- tourist numbers and revenue
- indices of production in major industrial groups
- estimated value of agricultural output
- construction output
- foreign trade
- main trading partners
- balance of payments
- trends in national debt
- servicing of external Government debt
- official external reserves
- average annual exchange rates

Economist Intelligence Unit (EIU)
COUNTRY REPORT: Ireland
London: Economist Intelligence Unit (quarterly)

The EIU *Country Report: Ireland* gives an appraisal of the economic situation and prospects for the economy. It comments on:

- economic policy
- Gross Domestic Product (GDP) growth
- Government finances and Exchequer Borrowing Requirement (EBR)
- manufacturing industry and industrial production
- retail sales volume
- new car registrations
- housing starts and completions
- labour force, employment/unemployment
- inflation
- prices (consumer prices, manufacturing prices)
- average hourly earnings in manufacturing
- foreign trade
- balance of payments
- exchange rates
- interest rates
- money supply
- monetary indicators
- business news.

Economist Intelligence Unit (EIU)
WORLD OUTLOOK: forecasts of political and economic trends in over 180 countries
London: Economist Intelligence Unit (annually)

The EIU *World Outlook* gives:

- short-term forecasts of economic trends
- summary of international political and economic developments
- world economy (economic indicators, GDP growth, consumer prices, export prices, interest rates, exchange rates)
- fiscal policy (United States, Japan, European Union)
- monetary policy
- global economic prospects
- summary review for each country based on the more detailed *Country Reports*.

National Institute of Economic and Social Research (NIESR)
NATIONAL INSTITUTE ECONOMIC REVIEW (NIER)
London: National Institute of Economic and Social Research (quarterly)

Each issue of the *National Institute Economic Review* contains a section of the world economy which has an appraisal and forecast. Text and tables provide information on:

- output and GDP growth in OECD countries
- prices: commodity prices and consumer prices

- interest rates, exchange rates and their influence on investment
- trade: volume and value
- balance of payments
- individual OECD countries: an appraisal of the economic situation in each and short-term outlook
- prospects for Europe
- prospects for economic and monetary union
- economic growth and productivity.

Publications: International Organisations

European Communities, Commission

EUROPEAN ECONOMY + Supplements A, B and C
Luxembourg: Office for Official Publications of the European Communities (two issues and three reports per year)

European Economy contains important communications from the Commission to the Council and to Parliament on the economic situation and developments in the European Union. A detailed Statistical Annex is included in each issue. Examples of topics covered are:

- macro-economic policy mix conducive to growth and employment
- economic policy guidelines
- price and exchange rate stability
- labour market reforms
- public finance and EU budget
- economic outlook, growth prospects and employment trends
- economic situation and policy issues in the individual Member States.

Supplement A – Economic trends (11 issues per year)
This comprises text, tables and graphs on the Community economic outlook, industrial production, inflation, consumer prices, gross fixed capital formation, exports, private consumption, interest rates, foreign trade, labour costs, employment, manufacturing industry, numbers of unemployed, General Government receipts, expenditure and lending, balance on current account, etc.

Supplement B – Business and consumer survey results (11 issues per year)
This gives the main results of opinion surveys of chief executives (orders, stocks, production outlook) and of consumers (economic and financial situation and outlook), international indicators and consumer confidence indicators. Tables give international indicators, indicators of confidence, indicators for world economic growth, production expectations, order books, price expectations, construction industry confidence indicators.

Supplement C – Economic reform monitor (4 issues per year)
This provides brief overviews of economic developments and progress of reform in the countries of Central Europe, Russia and Ukraine, with which the EU has negotiated agreements.

European Communities, Commission
GENERAL REPORT ON THE ACTIVITIES OF THE EUROPEAN UNION
Luxembourg: Office for Official Publications of the European Communities (annually)

This has information on a wide range of issues. Those relevant to economic policy, economic development, financial and monetary matters may be summarised as:

- general economic situation in the Community
- industrial policy
- enterprise policy, distributive trades, tourism and support measures for businesses
- regional policy
- European Regional Development Fund (ERDF)
- monetary policy
- agricultural policy – reform of the Common Agricultural Policy (CAP), farm prices, quality of agricultural products
- fisheries policy – development of resources, bilateral agreements, market organisation
- customs, tariff and trade measures
- energy policy – internal energy market and individual sectors (oil, natural gas, solid fuels, electricity)
- transport – development of the Common Transport Policy; inland, sea and air transport.

A diary of principal events is also included.

European Communities, Eurostat (Statistical Office of the EC)
BASIC STATISTICS OF THE EUROPEAN UNION
Luxembourg: Office for Official Publications of the European Communities (annually)

This booklet contains statistical tables; those relevant to the economic situation are as follows.

General statistics of the EU

National accounts
GDP at market prices; volume indices of GDP at market prices; cost structure of GDP at market prices; final consumption of households per inhabitant, by purpose; gross fixed capital formation by product; taxes and social contributions; general Government net lending and borrowing

Regional accounts

Finance
Money market rates; conversion rates; Central Government debt; money supply (ECU); money supply: M1 (national currencies); financial market rates (yearly averages); index of share prices; foreign official reserves; balance of payments by main-heading balance

Balance of payments

Prices

Consumer price index

Population
By area; age and sex; marriages and deaths

Employment
Employment; unemployment; unemployment rates; employees by economic activity

Social protection
Current expenditure on social protection as percentage of GDP at market prices; current expenditure on social protection per inhabitant

Wages and salaries
Indices of real wages in industry (average gross hourly earnings of manual workers); hourly labour costs in industry; structure of labour costs in industry; average gross hourly earnings in agriculture

Industrial production
General indices of industrial production; production of various commodities, motor vehicles, merchant vessels; production of cotton and woollen yarns and fabrics; production of wood pulp, paper and board; production of tobacco; building: number of dwellings completed

Consumption

Energy
Production of primary energy; production of natural gas, electrical energy; consumption of energy; energy trade; imports of energy products

Agriculture, forestry and fisheries
Land use; production of cereals, milk, meat; yields of principal crops; livestock numbers

Consumption
Consumption of animal and vegetable products

Supply balance sheets

Agricultural holdings

Prices
EU indices of agricultural prices

Agricultural accounts

Forestry accounts

Fisheries
Catches by fishing region; trade; consumption; average prices of certain species

Trade
Imports/exports; volume indices; unit value indices; the EU's share of the main non-member countries' trade

Transport
Railways, passengers carried, rail freight traffic; inland waterways; maritime fleets; merchant shipping; length of roads; motor vehicles in use; road traffic accidents

Tourism

European Communities, Eurostat (Statistical Office of the EC)
EUROSTATISTICS: Data for short-term analysis
Luxembourg: Office for Official Publications of the European Communities (monthly)

This complements the other two Eurostat publications, *Basic Statistics of the Community* and *Eurostat Review*. It is designed to give the latest statistical data on the European Union as a whole, each Member State, the United States and Japan. Charts and graphs precede the tables, which contain figures for:

- national accounts
- employment – employees by category of economic activity (agriculture, manufacturing industry, service industry, etc.)
- unemployment (rates for men and women)
- industrial production (total production, production by category, production by activity)
- industrial producer price index
- energy (indices of production for coal, natural gas, crude oil, petroleum, electricity, nuclear energy)
- indices of consumption
- retail trade
- tourism
- agricultural products (beef, veal, pork, butter, skimmed milk powder)
- external trade (intra-EU trade, extra-EU trade and extra-EU trade by partner country)
- consumer prices indices
- purchase prices of the means of agricultural production
- exchange rates
- interest rates
- monetary aggregates (money supply)
- index of share prices
- balance of payments.

European Communities, Eurostat (Statistical Office of the EC)
EUROSTAT YEARBOOK
Luxembourg: Office for Official Publications of the European Communities (annually)

This gives a general picture of the economic and social situation in the EU Member States, United States of America, Canada and Japan. Charts, graphs and maps accompany the tables. Examples are as follows.

Population
- population and population increase
- people by age group
- vital statistics

Labour market
- employment rates (men, women and part-time workers)
- unemployment (numbers unemployed – men and women)
- long-term unemployed people
- earnings
- weekly working hours

Social protection
- social security benefits
- family allowances
- unemployment and old-age benefits

Consumption and spending
- total consumption
- consumption of products
- consumption of goods and services

Housing
- housing standards
- households by number of rooms
- distribution of household income

Land and the environment
- area and population density
- woodlands and inland waters
- agricultural area

National income and expenditure
- economic growth (Gross Domestic Product)
- output by industry (manufacturing, agriculture, forestry, fisheries, building and construction, service industries, etc.)
- Government receipts and expenditure

Consumer prices and interest rates
- cost of living comparisons in the EU
- exchange rates
- interest rates

Trade
- trade in goods and services

Transport

Tourism

European Communities, Eurostat (Statistical Office of the EC)
REGIONS – Statistical Yearbook
Luxembourg: Office for Official Publications of the European Communities (annually)

This contains tables accompanied by maps for the different regions in the EU Member States. The tables are grouped in the sections summarised below.

Demography
- average population
- population by age
- vital statistics

Population activity and unemployment
- labour force by age
- principal characteristics of activity
- unemployment

Economic aggregates
- gross value added at market prices
- gross value added at factor cost (by branch)
- total employment (by branch)
- wage and salary earners (by branch)

Agriculture
- land use
- areas harvested and yields
- livestock (numbers of cows, pigs, sheep, goats, etc.)
- agricultural accounts
- structure of agricultural holdings

Energy
- production of coal, gas, crude oil
- electricity output

Transport
- transport networks
- flows of goods by road, rail and waterways
- air and sea transport

Living standards

International Monetary Fund (IMF)
IRELAND – RECENT ECONOMIC DEVELOPMENTS
Washington, D.C.: International Monetary Fund (biannually)

This report comprises text, charts, graphs and tables and gives an assessment of recent economic developments in Ireland. Coverage includes:

- manufacturing output and performance
- indices for competitiveness
- employment and unemployment
- labour costs
- Government finances and budgetary developments
- Exchequer Borrowing Requirement (EBR)
- public debt and Official External Reserves
- interest rates
- inflation
- exchange rate developments
- national accounts and distribution of national income
- saving and investment
- consumer and wholesale price indices
- foreign trade
- medium-term outlook.

International Monetary Fund (IMF)
WORLD ECONOMIC OUTLOOK
Washington, D.C.: International Monetary Fund (biannually)

World Economic Outlook comprises text, tables and charts and contains information on:

- global economic prospects and policies (industrial countries, developing countries, transition countries)
- world economic situation and short-term prospects
- fiscal policies and trends in industrial countries
- fiscal challenges facing industrial countries
- foreign exchange markets
- balance of payments statistics
- foreign trade statistics
- external debt and debt service
- exchange rates
- interest rates
- key economic indicators.

Organisation for Economic Co-operation and Development (OECD)
ECONOMIC SURVEYS
Paris: OECD (annually)

The OECD publishes economic surveys for each member country. The *Economic Survey: Ireland* contains text and tables and has information on:

- performance of the Irish economy
- recent economic developments
- short-term projections
- demand and output
- major foreign investments in Ireland
- labour market developments
- labour force by status (employment structure, employment by occupation, unemployment, long-term unemployment, numbers of unemployed people by age, gender and marital status)
- budgetary developments
- monetary policy
- fiscal policy
- taxation
- financial markets
- balance of payments
- competition policy
- foreign trade
- social security contributions
- Government revenue and expenditure
- Exchequer Borrowing Requirement (EBR)
- wages
- consumer price increases.

Each issue contains a fold-out table entitled 'Basic statistics: international comparisons'. Figures are given for population, employment, Gross Domestic Product (GDP), gross fixed capital formation, Government expenditure and receipts, indicators of living standards, wages and prices, foreign trade, total official reserves.

Organisation for Economic Co-operation and Development (OECD)
MAIN ECONOMIC INDICATORS
Paris: OECD (monthly)

Each issue of the *Main Economic Indicators* comprises tables and graphs and is divided into two principal sections.

Indicators by subject
Gross Domestic Product (GDP), industrial production and leading indicators, construction, passenger cars, retail sales, prices (consumer and wholesale), hourly earnings, employment, unemployment, money supply, interest rates, exchange rates, share prices, world trade, foreign trade (OECD countries), national accounts, consumer price indices

Indicators by country
Gross Domestic Product (GDP), industrial production, business surveys i.e. orders, order books level, construction (dwellings completed), cost of construction, retail sales, employment, unemployment, wages, prices (consumer and wholesale), interest rates, share prices, foreign trade (imports/exports), balance of payments.

Organisation for Economic Co-operation and Development (OECD)
OECD ECONOMIC OUTLOOK
Paris: OECD (biannually, July and December)

The *OECD Economic Outlook* comprises text, tables, charts and graphs and is set out in four principal sections.

OECD economic outlook and policies
General assessment of the economic situation, macroeconomic policy management, medium-term fiscal policy, international trade developments, interest rates, etc.

Developments in individual OECD member countries
- present economic situation and prospects
- private consumption
- Government consumption
- imports/exports of goods and services
- GDP at market prices
- industrial production
- General Government financial balance
- unemployment rate
- household saving ratio
- economic and fiscal policies

Developments in selected non-OECD countries

Annex

Organisation for Economic Co-operation and Development (OECD)
OECD IN FIGURES: Statistics on the Member Countries – supplement to the *OECD Observer*
Paris: OECD (annually)

This aims to give a picture of the economies of the OECD member countries and the extent of the structural adjustment within them. Tables contain figures for:

- demography (numbers, growth rate, age structure of population as % of total population)
- employment (total labour force, numbers engaged in agriculture, forestry, fishing, industry, services, part-time employment as % of total employment, unemployment rates, long-term unemployment, % of youth labour force)
- capital (gross fixed capital formation, business sector capital output ratio, share prices (1990 = 100), commercial banks' % of average balance-sheet total)
- investment (direct investment flows)
- money (exchange rate currency units, purchasing power parities for GDP, consumer prices, money supply, interest rates, total Official Reserves
- energy – primary energy supply (nuclear, coal, oil, natural gas)
- energy – production and consumption
- National Product (Gross Domestic Product at market prices, gross fixed capital formation, private and Government consumption, trade balance, net national saving)
- sectoral contributions (agriculture, manufacturing industry, service industries, transport, public sector)
- taxation (total tax receipts, taxes, social security contributions, tax rates, disposable income of average production worker as % of gross pay)
- trade (imports/exports, goods and services, trade by commodities)
- tourism (tourist arrivals, nights in accommodation, tourist receipts and expenditure).

Organisation for Economic Co-operation and Development (OECD)
OECD OBSERVER
Paris: OECD (fortnightly)

Each issue has a section entitled 'Economic indicators'. Key indicators for each OECD member country include:

- Gross Domestic Product (GDP)
- consumer price index
- current balance
- unemployment rate
- interest rates.

Various issues of the *Observer* contain articles relevant to the economic situation, such as agriculture, economic development, labour market, employment outlook, income distribution, social welfare, investment, energy production, fishing industry, tourism.

United Nations. Department for Economic and Social Information and Policy Analysis
MONTHLY BULLETIN OF STATISTICS
New York: United Nations (monthly)

The *Monthly Bulletin of Statistics* updates the *Statistical Yearbook* described below and contains similar information. In addition, each month a different selection of special tables is presented, showing annual and/or quarterly data on a variety of subjects illustrating important economic long-term trends and developments. The tables contain figures for:
- population (birth, death and marriage rates)
- manpower (employment, unemployment, hours of work in manufacturing)

- forestry
- industrial production
- manufacturing industries (textiles, paper and paper products, rubber products, etc.)
- building materials (cement production)
- metals (production of pig-iron, crude steel, copper, tin, lead, zinc)
- electricity production
- foreign trade
- prices (export price index numbers, consumer price index numbers)
- finance (exchange rates, money supply, international reserves, gold reserves, Government bonds, market prices of industrial shares, rates of discount of central banks, money market rates)
- transport equipment.

United Nations. Department for Economic and Social Information and Policy Analysis
STATISTICAL YEARBOOK
New York: United Nations (annually)

The *Statistical Yearbook* mainly comprises tables; those relevant to the economic situation are:

- index numbers of agricultural production and production of various commodities (ten-year period)
- livestock numbers
- fish catches
- production of fertilisers
- timber production
- manufacturing industries (food, beverages and tobacco, textile and leather industries, paper, cement, metals, chemicals, etc.)
- labour force statistics (employment, unemployment by industry)
- wages (earnings in industry)
- prices (producer prices, consumer price index numbers)
- national accounts
- financial statistics (rates of discount of central banks, money market rates)
- population statistics
- foreign trade
- balance of payments
- energy (production, trade and consumption of commercial energy)
- transport (railway traffic, passengers carried, motor vehicles in use, merchant shipping fleets).

United Nations. Economic Commission for Europe (ECE)
ECONOMIC BULLETIN FOR EUROPE
New York: United Nations (annually)

This contains:

- a summary view of the ECE economies every year
- the economic situation in the ECE region for the year under review
- the current economic situation in Western Europe and North America (demand; Gross Domestic Product (GDP), costs and prices; labour market; external balances; monetary conditions; fiscal policy, short-term outlook)

- the transition economies (output and demand; employment and unemployment; costs and prices; macroeconomic policies and short-term outlook)
- foreign trade of the transition economies
- external financial developments in the transition economies
- foreign trade between the European Union and Eastern European countries
- statistical appendix – selected tables
- Western Europe and North America figures (15-year period) for real GDP; real private consumption; real public consumption; gross domestic fixed capital formation; total domestic demand; exports of goods and services; imports of goods and services; industrial output; total employment; unemployment rates
- transition countries' figures (15-year period) for Gross Domestic Product (GDP); gross industrial output; imports/exports; balance of trade; foreign trade by direction.

United Nations. Economic Commission for Europe (ECE)
ECONOMIC SURVEY OF EUROPE
New York: United Nations (annually)

This is prepared by the Secretariat of the Economic Commission for Europe in Geneva and comprises text, tables and charts. It covers the following topics.

The current economic situation in the ECE economies and the short-term outlook

The Western market economies
- expectations and outcomes
- output and the components of demand
- labour markets (employment, unemployment and labour market policy)
- costs and prices (world commodity prices, domestic costs and prices)
- external balances
- monetary policy and monetary conditions (long-term and short-term interest rates, exchange rates)
- fiscal policy
- short-term economic outlook
- changes in real GDP in the developed market economies
- industrial output
- foreign trade

The transition economies (Eastern Europe and the Baltic States)
This section has similar information to that given for the Western market economies.

Energy

Official Publications

Department of Foreign Affairs
DEVELOPMENTS IN THE EUROPEAN UNION
Dublin: Stationery Office (biannually)

In accordance with Section 5 of the 1972 European Communities Act, the Government is required to submit twice yearly to each House of the Oireachtas a report on the developments in the European Communities. Topics relevant to energy policy include:

- energy situation in the Community
- measures to maintain stocks
- natural gas supplies and the oil refining industry
- opening of 32% of the electricity market to competition
- nuclear safety.

Department of Transport, Energy and Communications*
ANNUAL REPORT AND FINANCIAL STATEMENTS
Dublin: Department of Transport, Energy and Communications (annually)

The Secretary's Review assesses the role of the Department and the performance of the relevant sectors.

Energy sector – new developments
- progress on common rules for the Internal Market in gas
- political agreement on the ratification by the Communities of the Energy Charter Treaty
- adoption of the Directive establishing common rules for the Internal Market in electricity
- production of electricity, peat and gas
- oil supplies and the Whitegate Oil Refinery

* Since July 1997 Department of Enterprise, Trade and Employment.

Other Publications: Irish

Bord na Móna
ANNUAL REPORT
Dublin: Bord na Móna (annually)

Bord na Móna was established in 1946 to develop the country's peat resources. It supplies the industrial and domestic market with briquettes and machine turf. It produces peat fuel for use in the Electricity Supply Board's peat-burning power stations, moss peat for horticultural use and a variety of peat products for a world-wide market.

The *Annual Report* reviews the Board's operations, planned investment and development plans, projected output, pricing policy and the peat industry's contribution to the national economy.

Text, tables, graphs and charts cover:

* bog development – drainage and turf production
* location and output of works
* production – machine turf, milled peat, briquettes and moss peat
* sales and sales revenue – turf supplied for electricity generation and exports expressed in IR£ millions.

The *Annual Report* also includes the Financial Statements and organisation and structure of the Board.

Bord Gáis Éireann – The Irish Gas Board
ANNUAL REPORT AND ACCOUNTS
Little Island, Co. Cork: Bord Gáis Éireann (annually)

Bord Gáis Éireann is a statutory body established in 1976. Its principal function is to acquire and distribute natural gas from the Kinsale Head gas field to various parts of the country. When this supply diminishes, natural gas will have to be brought in via the interconnector pipeline.

The Chairman's Statement and the Chief Executive's Review comment on:

* performance of Bord Gáis Éireann
* investment in the gas network programme
* Ireland's primary energy demand
* gas deliveries (domestic, industrial/commercial, and deliveries to Nitrigin Éireann Teoranta (NET) and to the Electricity Supply Board (ESB)
* promotion of Combined Heat and Power (CHP) for the development of more efficient energy uses.

Electricity Supply Board (ESB)
ANNUAL REPORT
Dublin: Electricity Supply Board (annually)

The ESB is a State-sponsored body and was established under the Electricity (supply) Act 1927.

The Chairman's Statement and Chief Executive's Review comment on:

* the operation of the ESB
* investment and development plans
* projected output from its generating stations
* pricing policy
* restructuring the electricity industry
* activities of the Treasury function
* review of the finances of the ESB
* financial performance and competitiveness.

Irish National Petroleum Corporation
ANNUAL REPORT
Dublin: Irish National Petroleum Corporation (annually)

The Irish National Petroleum Corporation is a private limited company wholly owned by the Minister for Enterprise, Trade and Employment.

The Chairman's Statement comments on:
- performance of the company and its purchases of crude oil
- refining of crude oil, refining margins, a decline in the demand for gasoline
- increased demand for diesel fuel, jet fuel and kerosene
- Government investment programmes in the refineries at Whitegate and Whiddy Island
- crude oil prices, commercial oil stocks, refinery crude oil throughput (1993–1997), operating costs

The Director's Report comments on:
- the principal activities of the Corporation
- trading conditions, value of petroleum stocks and refining margins.

Publications: International Organisations

European Communities, Commission
ENERGY IN EUROPE – Annual Energy Review
Luxembourg: Office for Official Publications of the European Communities (annually)

This comprises text and statistical tables. Coverage includes the world, Western Europe, European Union, EFTA countries, Central and Eastern Europe, Russia, Asia, Africa, United States, Latin America, Canada.

Information is given on:

- the energy situation and outlook
- energy production
- consumption and energy demand
- imports of solid fuels, oil petroleum products, natural gas, etc.

European Communities, Commission
ENERGY IN EUROPE: Energy Policies and Trends in the European Community
Luxembourg: Office for Official Publications of the European Communities (biannually)

Energy in Europe contains information on:
- EU energy policy
- energy trends in the EU
- Community legislation in the energy sector
- market for different types of fuels
- environmental performances of power generating stations
- energy co-operation between the EU and other European countries
- trends in energy consumption
- energy supplies and prospects
- investment in energy projects
- production of gas, electricity, coal, nuclear energy, hydro-electricity, etc.
- employment and competitiveness in the energy sector.

Some issues of *Energy in Europe* carry a special feature such as:
- compendium of legislation and other instruments relating to energy

- European Community gas supply and prospects.

European Communities: Eurostat (Statistical Office of the EC)
ENERGY – Monthly Statistics
Luxembourg: Office for Official Publications of the European Communities (monthly)

This bulletin comprises tables which give figures for:
- energy production from natural sources (coal, oil, natural gas), production of nuclear energy, hydroelectric energy and geothermal heat
- imports/exports
- gross inland consumption.

European Communities, Eurostat (Statistical Office of the EC)
ENERGY – Yearly Statistics
Luxembourg: Office for Official Publications of the European Communities (annually)

Energy – Yearly Statistics (previously entitled *Energy Statistics Yearbook*) brings together harmonised statistical information on the energy situation in the European Union.

The yearbook comprises tables which contain data on the following:

Energy indicators for each individual EU Member State
- production/consumption by industry, households and the transport sector
- imports – fuel and oil price indices

Principal aggregates by product
- production (hard coal, lignite, peat, crude oil, natural gas, nuclear heat, hydroelectricity)
- imports/exports
- consumption of energy products (petroleum products, natural gas, electricity, fuel oil, motor spirit, diesel oil)

World energy production and reserves
This table gives figures for the production and reserves of hard coal, crude oil, natural gas in respect of the world, Europe, Africa, America, Far East, Middle East, Asia and Oceania.

European Communities, Eurostat (Statistical Office of the EC)
ENERGY BALANCE SHEETS
Luxembourg: Office for Official Publications of the European Communities (annually)

Explanatory notes and conversion coefficients precede the tables in this bulletin. Coverage includes all the EU Member States.

Balance sheet information
- primary production of solid fuels, crude oil, LPG (liquid petroleum gas), motor fuels, jet fuels, naptha, diesel oil
- input by type of fuel by power stations
- output by thermal power stations, nuclear power stations, coke-oven plants, blast furnace plants, gas works and refineries
- energy consumption by:

- branches of industry (metal industry, chemical industry, food and drink, textile and clothing, paper and printing, building and engineering industries)
- transport (railways, road traffic, air traffic and inland navigation)
- households, commerce, public authorities, etc.

European Communities, Eurostat (Statistical Office of the EC)
ENERGY PRICES
Luxembourg: Office for Official Publications of the European Communities (annually)

Energy Prices 1980–1996, published in 1997, comprises statistical tables which give price indices in national currencies for:

- natural gas (households and industry)
- electricity (domestic and industrial)
- heating oil (household consumption)
- residual fuel oil (consumption by industry)
- premium gasoline
- premium unleaded gasoline
- diesel oil
- comparison between energy prices.

European Communities, Eurostat (Statistical Office of the EC)
ENERGY PRICES
Luxembourg: Office for Official Publications of the European Communities (annually)

This bulletin comprises tables which contain figures for:

- consumer prices for gas, electricity and oil in the EU Member States
- prices of energy in national currencies and ECU (European currency unit)
- comparative energy prices for the industrial and household sectors

Detailed information on prices is published by the European Commission in:
- *Oil Price Bulletin* (weekly)
- *Statistics in Focus for Gas and Electricity* (biannually)
- *Gas Prices and Electricity Prices* (annually).

International Energy Agency (IEA)
COAL INFORMATION
Paris: OECD (annually)

The International Energy Agency (IEA) was established as an autonomous body in 1974 within the framework of the OECD to implement an International Energy Programme. The IEA also carries out a comprehensive programme of energy co-operation among the OECD member countries. Its objectives precede the table of contents in each issue.

Coal Information has been published annually since 1983. The 1995 report was published in 1996 and comprises three parts.

Part 1: World coal market

- developments in the world coal market
- overview of the economic situation
- overview of the energy situation
- prices (steam coal, coking coal, hard coal)
- demand (steam coal, coking coal, hard coal)
- outlook for coal demand
- coal demand statistics
- trade (hard coal, steam coal, coking coal)
- outlook for world coal trade
- coal trade statistics
- developments in world coal supply
- changes in national coal policies
- outlook for coal supply
- developments in coal production, labour costs, coal resources
- environmental impact of coal usage

Part 2: Coal data

- OECD total
- OECD North America, OECD Pacific, OECD Europe, IEA total, IEA North America and each OECD member country:
  - energy consumption, GDP and population
  - total primary energy supply by fuel
  - final energy consumption by fuel
  - coal balance
  - consumption of coal for selected end-uses
  - coal production by fuel type
  - coal trade by type
  - coal (hard coal, coking coal, steam coal) imports by origin and exports by destination
  - fuel prices to end users.

Part 3: Non-OECD countries' coal data

International Energy Agency (IEA)
ENERGY BALANCES OF OECD COUNTRIES
Paris: OECD (annually)

Explanatory notes precede the tables, charts and graphs for each OECD member country. The bulletin contains the following.

Energy indicators and energy balance sheets for each OECD country

- energy production
- net imports of energy
- net oil imports
- total primary energy supply
- consumption/production of electricity
- total primary energy supply

Summary tables

- production of coal and other solid fuels
- production of crude oil

- production of natural gas
- production of nuclear energy
- net imports of energy
- electricity generation (from coal, oil, gas, hydro energy, nuclear energy)
- final consumption of coal, oil, gas, electricity
- total final consumption of energy
- industry consumption of coal, oil, gas, electricity
- consumption of energy in transport
- other sectors' consumption of coal, oil and gas

International Energy Agency (IEA)
ENERGY PRICES AND TAXES
Paris: OECD (quarterly)

Energy Prices and Taxes provides OECD country statistics on energy prices and taxes for all energy sources and main consuming sectors. It comprises three parts preceded by a summary.

Summary – Recent energy price developments and summary data
- prices in international trade
- taxes and duties
- end-use price indices

Part 1 – Import and export cost indices, trade regulations and duties
- crude oil spot prices
- oil product spot prices
- import costs of crude oil, natural gas, steam coal and coking coal
- export prices of steam coal and coking coal

Part 2 – Energy end-use prices in OECD countries
- indices of real energy end-use prices
- energy end-use prices, taxes and price indices in national currencies for each OECD member country
- taxation of energy prices
- energy end-use prices in US dollars for oil, diesel, gasoline, natural gas, coal, electricity, etc.

Part 3 – Energy end-use prices in non-OECD countries

International Energy Agency (IEA)
OIL AND GAS INFORMATION
Paris: OECD (annually)

This report commenced publication in 1989, replacing *Annual Oil and Gas Statistics. Oil and Gas Information 1995*, published in 1996, comprises four parts.

Part 1: Sources and definitions

Part 2: World oil and gas developments
- OECD energy consumption, oil demand and economic indicators
- world oil demand by country

- world demand by main product group
- OECD consumption of unleaded gasoline
- world crude oil and natural gas liquid (NGL) production
- world refinery output and capacity
- world oil ports
- world trade of crude oil and products
- IEA oil prices, crude imports, oil products and natural gas prices
- world natural gas production
- consumption and trade

Part 3: OECD oil data
- OECD total, OECD North America, OECD Pacific, OECD Europe, European Union member countries and each OECD member country
- oil supply and consumption
- supply of crude oil and natural gas liquid (NGL)
- motor gasoline – supply
- gas/diesel oil – supply and consumption
- fuel oil (residual) – supply and consumption
- imports by country of origin
- exports by country of destination

Part 4: OECD gas data
- OECD total, OECD North America, OECD Pacific, OECD Europe, European Union member countries and each OECD member country
- natural gas – supply and consumption
- natural gas imports by country of origin
- natural gas exports by country of destination.

International Energy Agency (IEA)
WORLD ENERGY OUTLOOK
Paris: OECD (annually)

Tables are preceded by text, charts and graphs; coverage includes:

- world energy demand and outlook
- demand for oil, natural gas, coal and electricity
- energy prices
- OECD oil imports
- world consumption of natural gas, oil, solid fuels.

Organisation for Economic Co-operation and Development (OECD)
ELECTRICITY SUPPLY IN OECD COUNTRIES
Paris: OECD (annually)

This comprises text, tables, charts and graphs, and has information on:

- developments in demand for electricity
- electricity generation (nuclear power, hydroelectricity, oil, natural gas, coal and solid fuels)
- electricity trade and market conditions

- output of power from generating stations
- carbon taxes.

United Nations. Department for Economic and Social Information and Policy Analysis
ENERGY STATISTICS YEARBOOK
New York: United Nations (annually)

The principal objective of the *Yearbook* is to provide a global framework of comparable data on long-term trends in the supply of mainly commercial primary and secondary forms of energy. Conversion factor tables and definitions precede the tables listed below.

- commercial energy – production, trade and consumption (oil, solid fuels, liquid fuels, natural gas, nuclear fuels)
- energy resources (fossil fuel, nuclear and hydraulic)
- electricity and heat (production, consumption, trade, capacity of electricity-generating plants – type)

Figures in the *Yearbook* are updated in the United Nations *Monthly Bulletin of Statistics.*

United Nations. Department for Economic and Social Information and Policy Analysis
STATISTICAL YEARBOOK
New York: United Nations (annually)

The *Statistical Yearbook* is international in scope. Countries are listed in alphabetical order. Figures for energy are contained in the tables encaptioned:

- production, trade and consumption of commercial energy
- production of selected energy commodities.

United Nations. Economic Commission for Europe (ECE)
ANNUAL BULLETIN OF COAL STATISTICS FOR EUROPE AND NORTH AMERICA
Geneva: United Nations (annually)

This is divided in two parts and mainly comprises graphs and tables.

Part 1
- an overview of the coal situation in Europe
- graphs:
  - production of hard coal, brown coal and coke in the world and ECE region (specific years)
  - hard coal consumption by user sector in the ECE region
  - production of electricity by fuel in the ECE region
  - main hard coal importers and exporters
- summary tables:
  - production, imports, exports and gross consumption of hard coal and brown coal
  - deliveries of hard and brown coal for electricity and steam production (specific years)
  - supply and demand forecast of hard coal for ECE countries

Part 2
- country tables:
  - balance sheet of solid forms of energy
  - hard and brown coal mines: structure of production, employment, and productivity of labour
  - imports and exports of solid fuel by country

United Nations. Economic Commission for Europe (ECE)
ANNUAL BULLETIN OF ELECTRIC ENERGY STATISTICS FOR EUROPE AND NORTH AMERICA
Geneva: United Nations (annually)

This is divided into two parts and mainly comprises graphs and tables preceded by explanatory notes.

Part 1
- an overview of the electric power and heat situation in the ECE
- graphs:
  - total gross consumption of electrical energy in the World and ECE
  - average per capita consumption of electric energy in the ECE member countries (13-year period)
  - production of electricity by fuel in the ECE
  - main importers and exporters of electrical energy
  - nuclear share of electricity generation in selected countries
  - exchanges of electricity
- summary tables:
  - gross electricity production and annual growth rate in the ECE region
  - gross electricity production by type of plant in the ECE region
  - electricity consumption by user sectors in the ECE region
  - production and projections of electricity in the ECE region, 1970–2010
  - production and consumption of electricity in ECE countries
  - final consumption of energy in the ECE region

Part 2
- country tables:
  - production, imports, exports and supplies to consumers
  - electricity consumption
  - maximum net electrical capacity of plants in continuous operation by type
  - consumption of fuels and corresponding production of electricity and heat
  - imports and exports of electric energy

United Nations. Economic Commission for Europe (ECE)
ANNUAL BULLETIN OF GAS STATISTICS FOR EUROPE AND NORTH AMERICA
Geneva: United Nations (annually)

This is divided in two parts and mainly comprises graphs and tables.

Part 1
- an overview of the gas situation in Europe
- graphs:

– gross inland consumption of primary energy for the ECE region
– production of natural gas in the world (certain years)
– production of natural gas in the ECE region
– natural gas consumption in the world and in the ECE region
– average per capita consumption of natural gas in the ECE member countries
– natural gas reserves in the world and in the ECE region
– main importing and exporting countries of natural gas
- summary tables:
  – production and gross consumption of natural gas (specific years)
  – natural gas consumption by user sector in the ECE region
  – deliveries of natural gas for electricity and steam production
  – production, imports, exports and consumption of natural gas in the ECE region
  – final consumption of energy in the ECE region

Part 2
- country tables:
  – production, imports, exports and consumption of natural gas
  – production, imports, exports and consumption of manufactured gas
  – imports and exports of natural gas by country of origin
  – imports and exports of liquid petroleum gas (LPG)
  – length of mains for transport and distribution of gas

United Nations. Economic Commission for Europe (ECE)
ANNUAL BULLETIN OF GENERAL ENERGY STATISTICS FOR EUROPE
Geneva: United Nations (annually)

This comprises statistical tables preceded by explanatory notes.

Tables
- production of energy by form
- overall energy balance sheet
- deliveries of petroleum products for inland consumption

FINANCE

Official Publications

Central Statistics Office
STATISTICAL ABSTRACT
Dublin: Stationery Office (annually)

Each issue of the *Statistical Abstract* contains a section on Banking. The tables are supported by an explanatory text. Examples from the 1996 *Statistical Abstract* are listed below.

Banking
- currency outstanding: notes and coins, 1992–1995
- currency outstanding: denominations of legal tender notes, 1993–1995
- Irish token coinage issued by the Central Bank of Ireland, 1993–1995
- monetary sector: consolidated balance sheet, 1994 and 1995
- Central bank of Ireland: summary statement of assets and liabilities, 1993–1995
- all licensed banks: aggregate balance sheet *vis-à-vis* residents, 1993–1995
- all licensed banks: aggregate balance sheet *vis-à-vis* non-residents, 1993–1995

Post Office
- statement of business of Post Office Savings Bank, 1989–1995
- number and value of savings certificates issued, 1990–1995

Central Statistics Office
STATISTICAL ABSTRACT
Dublin: Stationery Office (annually)

Each issue of the *Statistical Abstract* contains a section on Public Finance. The tables are supported by an explanatory text. Examples from the 1996 *Statistical Abstract* are:

- Exchequer receipts, 1993–1995
- Exchequer issues, 1993–1995
- issues from the Exchequer for supply services, 1993–1996
- statement of State capital assets, 1992–1995
- Public Capital Programme, 1992–1995
- current Budget deficit and the Exchequer and public sector borrowing requirements, 1977–1996
- expenditure of Central Govenment classified by purpose of expenditure and economic category, 1990–1994
- receipts and expenditure of Central Government, 1990–1994
- net receipts from excise duties, 1991–1994
- value-added tax – registration by trade classification, 1991–1994
- income tax assessments and net tax due, 1991/92 and 1992/93.

Central Statistics Office
ECONOMIC SERIES
Dublin: Stationery Office (monthly)

The *Economic Series* bulletin provides up-to-date information and five years' retospection for a selection of 151 principal short-term economic series. Longer retrospection is given in each December issue.

Charts and graphs accompany the tables. Listed below are the numbers pertaining to monetary developments, interest rates, exchange rates and savings.

Monetary
8.10   Official external reserves
8.11   Bank debits – current account
8.12   Money supply M1
8.13   Money supply M3
8.14   Total currency in circulation

Interest rates
8.15   Central Bank short-term facility
8.16   Exchequer bills (91 day) average yield (per cent per annum)
8.17   Building society mortgage loans

Exchange rates
8.18   Sterling
8.19   US dollar
8.20   Deutsche mark
8.21   Effective rates

Savings
8.22   Building Society deposits
8.23   Post Office Savings Bank and Trustee Savings Banks
8.24   Price Index of Ordinary Stocks and Shares (ISEQ)

Department of the Environment*
RETURNS OF LOCAL TAXATION (year) with summary figures for the following years
Dublin: Stationery Office (annually)

This bulletin mainly comprises statistical tables preceded by an outline of the Local Government system.

Tables give figures for the following.

All local authorities
- revenue accounts – summary
- revenue accounts – receipts and expenditure
- revenue accounts – total receipts for all Local Authority programmes classified by source

County Councils/County Borough Corporations/Urban District Councils
- population, area, valuation, total revenue accounts, receipts and expenditure, and rate in the £
- revenue accounts – total receipts for all Local Authority programmes classified by source
- revenue accounts – receipts and expenditure
- revenue accounts – individual Local Authority programme receipts classified by source
- capital accounts – receipts, expenditure and indebtedness

Town Commissioners
- population, area, valuation, rate in the £ for town charges and capital account receipts, expenditure and indebtedness
- revenue accounts – receipts and expenditure

Miscellaneous bodies
- revenue accounts – receipts and expenditure

* Since July 1997 Department of the Environment and Local Government.

Department of Finance
BUDGET
Dublin: Stationery Office (annually)

The Budget is one of the principal sources of financial information. Some sections are published separately as booklets, as described below.

Financial statement of the Minister for Finance (also published separately)
Covers matters such as the economic situation, incomes policy, the national debt, Exchequer Borrowing Requirement (EBR), public expenditure, inflation, social welfare, public service pay, taxation (corporation tax, income tax, PRSI and levies, capital acquisitions tax, farmer taxation), review of Budget outturn.

Principal features of the Budget (also published separately)
The tables contain figures for:
- social welfare increases
- PRSI contributions
- summary of adjustments to non-capital supply services – net estimates
- details of main Budget adjustments from non-capital supply services
- gross current supply expenditure – year-on-year increase
- details of Budget Day adjustments to capital expenditure
- Local Authority financing
- tax changes and their revenue effects.

Financial resolutions

Economic background to the Budget (also published separately)
- summary of current economic situation and outlook for the economy
- review of the previous year (international economy and domestic developments)
- international economic prospects
- outlook for the Irish economy
- international trade
- balance of payments
- economic growth
- employment/unemployment
- earnings and competitiveness

Budgetary tables and statistics (also published separately)
- summary of current and capital budgets together with projections
- macroeconomic forecast
- current revenue

- current expenditure – allocation
- trend in the current budget deficit
- Exchequer Borrowing Requirement (EBR)
- trend in national debt and in service of public debt
- trend in current Government expenditure

National accounts classification of Budget (also published separately)
- transactions of Central Government and extra-budgetary funds

Pre-Budget Tables (also published separately)
- Budget outturn
- current Government expenditure
- receipts and expenditure of the Exchequer and of Local Authorities 1973 onwards

Estimates of receipts and expenditure for the year ending 31 December... (White Paper) (also published separately)
Estimates of Receipts and Expenditure are prepared by the Government and presented to Dáil Éireann in accordance with the provisions of Article 28 of the Constitution.

Department of Finance
ECONOMIC REVIEW AND OUTLOOK
Dublin: Stationery Office (annually)

The appendix in the *Economic Review and Outlook* comprises statistical tables with comparative figures for approximately nine years. Tables relevant to finance are:

- Gross National Product and Gross Domestic Product at current market prices and percentage change in GNP and GDP at constant (1990) prices
- expenditure on GNP at current market prices
- expenditure on GNP at constant (1990) market prices
- GDP at factor cost by sector of origin and GNP at current market prices
- GDP at factor cost by sector of origin and GNP at constant (1990) market prices
- Net Domestic Product at factor cost by sector of origin and GNP at current market prices
- national income
- interest rates
- exchange rates
- national disposable income, savings and capital formation
- General Government deficit.

Department of Finance
ESTIMATES FOR PUBLIC SERVICES (abridged version) and SUMMARY PUBLIC CAPITAL PROGRAMME
Dublin: Stationery Office (annually)

Estimates for Public Services (abridged version) are presented to Dáil Éireann in accordance with the provisions of Article 28 of the Constitution. They are published a couple of months before the Budget Statement.

They comprise tables showing allocations of voted public expenditure for:

- the Public Service (i.e. the President's Establishment, Houses of the Oireachtas, Government Departments, Office of the Revenue Commissioners, Office of the Attorney General, Office of the Comptroller and Auditor General, Garda Síochána, Prisons, Courts, National Gallery, etc.)
- Remuneration and pensions
- Summary Public Capital Programme.

Department of Finance
FINANCE ACCOUNTS
Dublin: Stationery Office (annually)

The Department of Finance is required under statute to prepare and present to both Houses of the Oireachtas detailed annual accounts of the Central Fund. These accounts, known as the Finance Accounts, contain detailed analysis and classification of receipts and issues of the Central Fund as well as details relating to the National Debt.

The accounts are summarised below.

- Exchequer account – receipts, issues and balances
- revenue accounts (tax revenue and non-tax revenue)
- payments charged to the Central Fund in respect of annuities, pensions, salaries, allowances, etc.
- capital investments: repayable advances
- capital investments: State-sponsored bodies
- capital investments: international bodies
- capital receipts from the European Union
- guaranteed loans – nature of loan and amount outstanding
- annuities, pensions, etc. – to whom payable
- National Debt of Ireland – statement

Department of Finance
REVISED ESTIMATES FOR PUBLIC SERVICES
Dublin: Stationery Office (annually)

The *Revised Estimates for Public Services* are published after the Budget Statement. They comprise tables showing allocations of voted public expenditure with figures for expenditure changes announced by the Minister for Finance in his Financial Statement in the Budget speech:

- Public Service (i.e. The President's establishment, Houses of the Oireachtas, European Parliament, Government Departments, Office of the Revenue Commissioners, Office of the Attorney General, Office of the Comptroller and Auditor General, Garda Síochána, Prisons, Courts, National Gallery, etc.)
- increases in remuneration and pensions
- capital services.

Department of Foreign Affairs
DEVELOPMENTS IN THE EUROPEAN UNION
Dublin: Stationery Office (biannually)

In accordance with Section 5 of the 1972 European Communities Act, the Government is required to submit twice yearly to each House of the Oireachtas a report on the developments in the European Communities. Topics relevant to monetary policy and fiscal policy include:

- the Community Budget
- European Investment Bank loans
- European Investment Fund
- the European Monetary System (EMS)
- harmonisation of taxes
- Government deficits of EU Member States
- Ireland's Convergence Programmes
- EU loans for Ireland.

Houses of the Oireachtas
ACTS – Finance Act
Dublin: Stationery Office (annually)

The Finance Act is the principal source of information on taxation, duties and levies. It has information on:

- income tax
- taxation on farming profits
- corporation tax
- capital gains tax
- capital acquisitions tax
- customs duties
- excise duties
- value-added tax
- vehicle registration tax
- stamp duties
- tax reliefs.

Office of the Comptroller and Auditor General
ANNUAL REPORT OF THE COMPTROLLER AND AUDITOR GENERAL and APPROPRIATION ACCOUNTS
Dublin: Stationery Office (annually)

The Appropriation Accounts are prepared by Government Departments and Offices to meet statutory requirements which specify that each account must show how the amount set aside by the Oireachtas for the activities of those departments and offices in a given financial year was spent.

Appropriation Accounts: Public Services
Summary table shows: vote number, services, estimated expenditure (gross), estimated appropriations in aid, net supply grant, actual expenditure (gross), appropriations in aid realised, net expenditure, outturn (gross) compared with estimate, amount to be surrendered, Exchequer extra receipts (estimated and realised).

The votes
(The amount of money voted by Dáil Éireann for each Department or service.) In respect of each vote a breakdown is given showing the various services provided, estimate provision, outturn, closing accruals.

Registrar of Building Societies
REPORT OF THE REGISTRAR OF BUILDING SOCIETIES
Dublin: Stationery Office (annually)

This Report is published pursuant to section 86 of the Building Societies Act, 1976. The societies have been divided into three groups:

- societies with assets exceeding £100 million
- societies with assets over £25 million and up to £100 million
- societies with assets up to £25 million.

Tables give figures for:
- total assets
- breakdown of assets
- share and deposit transactions
- share and deposit holdings
- average shares and deposits
- mortgage advances
- amount and purposes of advances
- mortgages outstanding
- investments
- liquidity and reserves
- income and expenditure.

Registrar of Friendly Societies
REPORT OF THE REGISTRAR OF FRIENDLY SOCIETIES
Dublin: Stationery Office (annually)

This report is published pursuant to the Trade Union Act, 1871; Industrial and Provident Societies Act, 1893; Friendly Societies Act, 1896; Perpetual Funds (Registration) Act, 1933; Credit Union Act, 1966; and in accordance with the provisions of the Ministers and Secretaries Act, 1924.

Financial statistics are derived from the annual returns submitted by the societies.

Tables contain figures for:
- credit unions
  - numbers on the register
  - breakdown of assets and liabilities
  - breakdown of income and expenditure
- friendly societies
  - numbers on the register
  - assets and liabilities
  - advances made during the year
  - income and expenditure
- trade unions (various categories)
  - numbers on the register
  - income and expenditure
  - total amount in political funds

- industrial and provident societies (deposit-taking and non-deposit-taking)
  - numbers on the register

- income and expenditure
- assets and liabilities
- alphabetical list of societies on the register.

Revenue Commissioners

ANNUAL REPORT OF THE REVENUE COMMISSIONERS

Dublin: Stationery Office (annually)

The *Annual Report of the Revenue Commissioners* contains details of relevant legislation and receipts of revenue from various taxes and duties.

Figures are given for:
- total amount collected/gross receipts
- total revenue/net receipts
- income tax
- corporation tax
- capital acquisitions tax (CAT)
- capital gains tax
- value-added tax (VAT)
- levies (pay-related social insurance (PRSI), employment and training levy)
- customs and excise duties
- stamp duties.

Examples of other topics covered are tax evasion, customer services, the tax amnesty, decentralisation of the Office of the Revenue Commissioners, Revenue audit programmes and performance appraisal.

The Report also includes:
- the principal legislative changes during the year under review
- structure of the Board
- list of persons on whom fines were imposed
- list of persons relating to underpaid tax and the amount of settlement.

Revenue Commissioners

CUSTOMS AND EXCISE TARIFF OF IRELAND

Dublin: Stationery Office (annually)

Each edition of the *Customs and Excise Tariff of Ireland* sets out the customs duties chargeable on imported goods. It also sets out the excise duties chargeable. It incorporates the Tariff of the European Communities (TARIC).

Where information contained in Part 4 – Schedule of Duties is at variance with that contained in the relevant community legislation published in the *Official Journal of the European Communities*, the latter represents the correct legal position.

The tariff code number shown opposite each category of goods in the schedule of customs duties is also the statistical number for those goods.

Revenue Commissioners
STATISTICAL REPORT OF THE REVENUE COMMISSIONERS
Dublin: Stationery Office (annually)

The *Statistical Report* comprises text, charts and tables and contains detailed information on all the taxes and duties for which the Office of the Revenue Commissioners is responsible. The Report is set out under the following headings:

- total revenue
- excise duties
- stamp duties
- capital acquisitions tax
- residential property tax
- income tax, tax reliefs and tax allowances
- income distribution statistics
- corporation tax
- capital gains tax
- value-added tax (VAT)
- Sheriff and solicitor enforcement.

Other Publications: Irish

ACCBANK plc
ANNUAL REPORT and FINANCIAL STATEMENTS
Dublin: ACCBANK plc (annually)

ACCBANK plc is a State-sponsored bank. It provides a wide range of banking services to personal borrowers, the farming community and the business and corporate sectors. The *Annual Report* gives information on the following.

Principal services provided by the Bank
- retail banking (loans to the personal sector)
- treasury services
- corporate banking (agri-business, investment property, hotel finance, telecommunications, tax-based lending)

Organisation and structure of the Bank
The Chairperson's Statement and the Chief Executives Review:
- comment on the performance of the Bank
- comment on the economic outlook for the Bank and its customers
- review the Bank's activities.

Central Bank of Ireland
ANNUAL REPORT
Dublin: Central Bank of Ireland (annually)

In addition to the Statement of Accounts, the *Annual Report* gives an appraisal of the national economy and a short-term forecast. It also has information on the following.

The national economy
- expenditure on Gross National Product (GNP)

- price developments
- consumer spending
- fiscal developments
- Government expenditure and revenue
- Exchequer Borrowing Requirement (EBR)
- trade and balance of payments
- industrial production
- labour market – employment, unemployment and pay

Monetary and financial market developments
- money and credit
- monetary aggregates – annual rates of change
- change in money supply
- change in private-sector credit
- Irish pound exchange rates
- interest rate and bond-yield differentials
- sales of Government securities
- financing the Exchequer Borrowing Requirement (EBR)

International developments
- economic developments in the major economies such as the United States, Japan, Germany, France
- developments in the major currencies – US dollar, £ sterling, Japanese yen, German mark
- European Union, Exchange Rate Mechanism (ERM)
- three-month Euro-currency interest rates

Statistical appendix
- list of reporting institutions
- list of credit institutions
- list of authorised money brokers
- investment business firms authorised by the Central Bank
- main monetary indicators
- interest rates, exchange rates, balance of payments
- banking and financial institutions – assets and liabilities
- credit institutions and building societies – balance sheets
- transactions on the Irish Pound Forward Rate Agreement Market

Public finances
- Government debt
- servicing the national debt
- Government expenditure, revenue and borrowing
- Government saving schemes
- State-sponsored bodies – assets and liabilities

Economic indicators

All issues of the Central Bank of Ireland *Annual Report* and *Quarterly Bulletin* contain 'special articles'.

Central Bank of Ireland
IRISH ECONOMIC STATISTICS
Dublin: Central Bank of Ireland (annually)

Irish Economic Statistics is a fold-out booklet published annually with the autumn issue of the *Quarterly Bulletin*. The tables contain figures for the current year, previous year and previous tenth year, for the following.

National product
- consumer expenditure
- public current expenditure
- fixed investment
- exports/imports of goods and services

Industrial production
- mining and quarrying
- manufacturing industries
- chemicals
- metals and engineering
- food, drink and tobacco
- textile industry
- clothing, footwear and leather
- timber and wooden furniture
- paper and printing

Building and construction
- housing stock
- public capital expenditure
- output of building and construction industry

Agriculture
- gross agricultural product
- cattle numbers
- milk output

Manpower
- total labour force
- numbers unemployed
- numbers employed in agriculture and industry
- industrial disputes (total man-days lost through industrial disputes)

Income
- national income
- weekly earnings in industry (men and women)
- weekly hours worked (men and women)

Prices
- consumer price index
- wholesale price index
- import/export prices

External trade
- imports/exports

Balance of payments
- balance on current account
- net balance on capital and financial account
- official external reserves (end December)

Government finance
- current revenue (direct taxation, indirect taxation, non-tax revenue)
- current expenditure
- current Budget deficit (surplus)
- Exchequer Borrowing Requirement (EBR)
- external Government debt (end December)

Banking statistics
- currency
- narrow money supply
- wide money supply

Private sector credit
- licensed banks
- all credit institutions

Selected interest rates/yields (end year)
- Central Bank short-term facility
- Associated Banks' prime lending rate
- Interbank one-month fixed rate
- Associated Banks' deposit rate demand deposits
- building societies (investment share accounts; representative yield on Irish Government securities with five years to maturity, Equity Index)
- exchange rate (Irish pound against pound sterling, US dollar, Deutsche mark)

Indicators of living standards
- retail sales (volume)
- private motor cars
- new car registrations
- telephones and television sets

Central Bank of Ireland
MONTHLY STATISTICS
Dublin: Central Bank of Ireland (monthly)

Monthly Statistics comprises tables which update the figures in the tables in the *Quarterly Bulletin* and *Annual Report* of the Central Bank.

Central Bank of Ireland
QUARTERLY BULLETIN
Dublin: Central Bank of Ireland (quarterly)

The *Quarterly Bulletin* contains information similar to that given in the *Annual Report*, e.g. the following.

The national economy
- appraisal of the national economy
- consumer spending
- investment
- fiscal developments
- trade and balance of payments
- production – industry and services
- agricultural output and incomes
- labour market – employment and unemployment

Monetary and financial market developments
- monetary policy
- money and credit
- financial markets – exchange rates and interest rates
- Irish pound exchange rates
- financing the Exchequer Borrowing Requirement (EBR)

International developments
- economic developments in the major economies
- key economic indicators

Statistical appendix – selected tables
- main economic indicators
- interest rates, exchange rates and balance of payments
- public finances
- economic indicators

All issues of the Central Bank of Ireland *Annual Report* and *Quarterly Bulletin* contain special articles, such as:
- EMU and Irish monetary policy
- economic growth in Ireland: sources, potential and inflation
- inflational process in Ireland.

ICC Bank plc
ANNUAL REPORT and FINANCIAL STATEMENTS
Dublin: ICC Bank plc (annually)

In July 1992 the Industrial Credit Corporation plc changed its name to ICC Bank plc. It provides a wide range of financial services to the State and serves the financial needs of small and medium-sized businesses.

The *Annual Report* gives information on the following.

Principal services provided by the Bank
- loans (short-, medium-, long-term; fixed or variable)
- international trade services
- venture capital
- treasury services

- corporate finance
- mergers & acquisitions
- corporate valuations
- international consultancy

Organisation and structure of the Board of Directors

The Chairman's Review and the Directors' Report comment on:
- performance of the Bank
- medium-term economic outlook for the Bank and its customers
- Business Expansion Fund management
- allocation of funds for loans, drawn down from the European Investment Bank (EIB)
- the Bank's business strategy.

Irish Times plc
IRISH TIMES, THE
Dublin: Irish Times (daily Monday to Saturday)

Share prices quoted on the Irish Stock Exchange are published in *The Irish Times* and companies are listed in alphabetical order.

The London closing prices are quoted in sterling and the companies are grouped in various categories, such as banks; brewing/catering; building; chemicals; electricity; electronic/electrical; engineering; extractive industries; food producers; household, textile; leisure and hotels; life assurance; media; oil exploration; paper, printing; pharmaceuticals; retailers; telecommunications; transport; water.

Exchange rates are published for the Irish pound and for Sterling against all the major currencies.

National Treasury Management Agency
ANNUAL REPORT AND ACCOUNTS
Dublin: National Treasury Management Agency (annually)

The National Treasury Management Agency was established under the Treasury Management Agency Act, 1990.

The *Annual Report* contains a brief account of the setting up of the Agency, its objectives and functions, summarised as follows:

- it borrows money for the Exchequer
- it manages the National Debt
- it raises funds for the Exchequer Borrowing Requirement (EBR)
- it refinances maturing and prepayable debt.

The Chief Executive reviews the performance of the Agency. The *Annual Report* also contains information on the national debt, debt service costs, trend in GNP and average interest rate, General Government debt to GDP ratios of EU member states, Ireland's debt position relative to EU average, Ireland's credit rating and debt management policy, National Savings Schemes, foreign currency debt portfolio, SWAPs activity, etc.

National Treasury Management Agency
IRELAND: INFORMATION MEMORANDUM
Dublin: National Treasury Management Agency (annually)

The *Information Memorandum* contains information on:
- public finance developments (budget deficit, Exchequer Borrowing Requirement)
- National Debt management
- main economic developments
- main economic indicators
- agriculture
- labour force
- employment/unemployment
- international trade
- balance of payments
- monetary policy
- average exchange rate of the Irish pound against selected currencies.

Terry Cooney, Jim McLaughlin, Joe Martin
TAXATION SUMMARY
Dublin: Institute of Taxation of Ireland (annually)

This is a detailed guide which covers:

- income tax
- corporation tax
- capital acquisitions tax
- probate tax
- value-added tax
- capital allowances
- stamp duties.

Each new edition includes the provisions of the latest Finance Act.

Other Publications: British

ECONOMIST, THE
London: Economist Newspaper Ltd (weekly)

In each issue financial indicators are published for most European countries, Japan and the United States.

Financial indicators
- stock markets – share price indices (high/low, one week/one year, in local currency, in US dollars)
- money and interest rates (money supply, interest rates % p.a., three-month money market, banks, bond yields, Eurocurrency)
- trade, exchange rates and reserves (trade balance ($bn), current account ($bn), exchange rate, currency units per $, foreign reserves ($bn)).

Tolley Publishing Company plc
TOLLEY'S TAXATION IN THE REPUBLIC OF IRELAND
Croydon: Tolley Publishing Co. (annually)

This is a detailed guide covering income tax, corporation tax, capital acquisitions tax, value-added tax and the provisions of the most recent Finance Act.

Publications: International Organisations

European Communities, Commission
THE COMMUNITY BUDGET: the Facts in Figures
Luxembourg: Office for Official Publications of the European Communities (annually)

The Community Budget: Facts in Figures 1997 comprises text, graphs, charts, maps and tables. It covers:

- the basic principles governing the Community Budget
- budgetary procedure
- a historical account of Community revenue and expenditure
- appropriations for payment
- comparison between the 1996 budget, 1997 financial perspective and 1997 budget
- the 1997 budget by subsection
- ECSC operating budget 1997
- European Development Fund (EDF) 1997
- preliminary draft budget for 1998.

European Communities, Commission
GENERAL BUDGET OF THE EUROPEAN UNION FOR THE FINANCIAL YEAR ... THE FIGURES
Luxembourg: Office for Official Publications of the European Communities (annually)

This comprises text, charts and tables, and gives:

- a breakdown of expenditure by subsection
- a general summary of appropriations for the previous and current year
- a breakdown by heading (i.e. Common Agricultural Policy (CAP), Structural Funds, Cohesion Funds, European Social Fund (ESF), Community Initiatives, etc.)
- administrative expenditure of the EU (i.e. the Commission, Parliament, Council, Court of Justice, Court of Auditors and the Economic and Social Committee)
- breakdown by type of revenue (i.e. levies and duties).

European Investment Bank (EIB)
ANNUAL REPORT
Luxembourg: Office for Official Publications of the European Communities (annually)

The European Investment Bank was established by the Treaty of Rome, 1958. Its members are the Member States of the European Union, which have all subscribed to its capital. It is an independent institution within the EU and its primary objective is to further the development of the Community.

The *Annual Report* of the EIB gives:

- an overview of the EIB's objectives and policies
- disbursement of funds, contracts signed and projects approved
- finance provided by the EIB within the EU
- breakdown of lending for each EU Member State (i.e. list of contracts signed, loans
- approved for each individual project, etc.)
- the EIB's financing terms and conditions
- operations of the Bank outside the European Union
- operations of the Bank within the European Union
- annual accounts and financial statements of the Bank
- structure and organisation of the EIB.

International Monetary Fund (IMF)
GOVERNMENT FINANCE STATISTICS YEARBOOK
Washington, D.C.: International Monetary Fund (annually)

This deals principally with Central Government finances. The world tables are arranged by topic and the country tables are in alphabetical order.

World tables
- Central Government income and expenditure
- Central Government debt (foreign and domestic)
- taxes on income and profits
- social security contributions
- grants as a percentage of total revenue
- expenditure on social security and social welfare as a percentage of total expenditure
- interest payments
- transfers to other levels of Government

Country tables
These contain the same type of information as the world tables.

International Monetary Fund (IMF)
INTERNATIONAL FINANCIAL STATISTICS YEARBOOK
Washington, D.C.: International Monetary Fund (annually)

The *International Financial Statistics Yearbook* is updated by monthly bulletins and comprises tables and charts, preceded by explanatory notes. The 1996 issue contains data for 133 countries for the years 1966 to 1995. World tables are followed by country tables as summarised below.

World Tables
Figures for:
- exchange rates
- fund accounts: position to date, all drawings
- international reserves
- international banking
- interest rates
- real effective exchange rate indices
- consumer prices

- industrial production
- wages
- employment
- international trade
- export/import unit values
- balance of payments
- commodity prices.

Country tables
Figures for:
- exchange rates (market rate and ECU rate)
- reserve position in the Fund (quota and SDRs)
- international liquidity
- deposit money banks: foreign assets and liabilities
- other financial institutions (assets and liabilities)
- prices (share prices, wholesale prices, consumer prices)
- wages: weekly earnings
- industrial production
- employment (manufacturing industry)
- international trade
- balance of payments
- Government finance
- national accounts
- population.

International Monetary Fund (IMF)
INTERNATIONAL FINANCIAL STATISTICS
Washington, D.C.: International Monetary Fund (monthly)

The monthly issues of *International Financial Statistics* update the *Yearbook* and comprise tables and charts preceded by explanatory notes. Country tables follow the world tables and cover approximately 133 countries. These monthly issues contain the same type of information as the *Yearbook*, described above.

Organisation for Economic Co-operation and Development (OECD)
FINANCIAL STATISTICS (issued in three parts)
Part 1 – Financial Statistics (monthly)
Part 2 – Financial Accounts by Country
Part 3 – Non-Financial Enterprises Financial Statements (irregularly)
Paris: OECD

Part 1 – Financial Statistics (monthly)

This bulletin is divided into two sections
Section 1: International markets
Section 2: Domestic markets – interest rates

Coverage includes: bond issues, medium and long-term bank loans on the international market and domestic markets and interest rates.

Part 2 – Financial Accounts by Country

The tables in this bulletin show Government finances, assets and liabilities of banking institutions, supply and demand for capital on the securities market, value of outstanding securities, etc.

Part 3 – Non-Financial Enterprises Financial Statements

The tables in this bulletin contain figures for: funds raised on the international market, official discount rates, interest rates, etc.

Organisation for Economic Co-operation and Development (OECD)
REVENUE STATISTICS
Paris: OECD (annually)

This bulletin provides comparative data from 1965 onwards, for the tax levels and tax structures which exist in OECD member countries. Explanatory notes, charts, graphs and code numbers precede the tables, arranged by country and by main heading with detailed subdivisions. Examples are listed below.

Comparative tables
- total tax revenue as percentage of GDP
- taxes on income and profits as percentage of GDP
- taxes on income and profits as percentage of total taxation
- taxes on personal income as percentage of total taxation
- taxes on corporate income as percentage of GDP
- social security contributions as percentage of GDP
- social security contributions as percentage of total taxation
- employee's social security contributions as percentage of GDP
- employee's social security contributions as percentage of total taxation
- employer's social security contributions as percentage of total taxation
- taxes on payroll and workforce as percentage of total taxation
- taxes on property as percentage of total taxation
- taxes on goods and services as percentage of GDP
- taxes on goods and services as percentage of total taxation
- consumption taxes as percentage of GDP
- total tax revenue in million dollars
- tax revenue in dollars per capita
- exchange rates used – national currency units per dollar

Country tables
- total tax revenue
- taxes on income, profits and capital gains
- consumption taxes as percentage of GDP
- consumption taxes as percentage of total taxation
- taxes on payroll and workforce
- taxes on goods and services
- taxes on property
- customs and excise duties
- levies – EU agriculture levies and bank levies

United Nations. Department for Economic and Social Information and Policy Analysis
STATISTICAL YEARBOOK
New York: United Nations (annually)

The *Statistical Yearbook* is international in scope. Countries are listed in alphabetical order. The tables for financial statistics are:

- rates of discount of central banks (ten-year period)
- short-term rates: Treasury bill and money market rates (ten-year period)
- exchange rates.

Housing/Building/Construction

Central Statistics Office
CENSUS OF POPULATION 1991. Volume 10 – Housing
Dublin: Stationery Office (approximately every five years)

This volume was published in February 1997. Explanatory notes precede the detailed statistical tables. Examples are as follows.

- persons in private and non-private households in each province, county and county borough
- permanent housing units classified by persons in private households, number of private households and number of rooms occupied by private households in aggregate town and aggregate rural areas of each province, county and county borough
- average number of persons per room in private households in permanent housing units in the aggregate town and aggregate rural areas of each province, county and county borough – 1946 to 1991
- private households in permanent housing units in each province and county classified by number of rooms occupied – 1946 to 1991
- persons in private households in permanent housing units, classified by number of persons per room in each province, county and county borough
- private dwellings classified by water supply, sanitary facilities, type of building in which situated and distinguishing number of persons in these dwellings
- private dwellings occupied by nature of occupancy
- rented private dwellings classified by weekly rent
- private dwellings in each planning region, classified by nature of occupancy, principal method of heating and principal type of fuel used
- farm dwellings in each province, county and county borough, period in which built, water supply and sanitary facilities

The questionnaire used to gather the information is included.

Central Statistics Office
ECONOMIC SERIES
Dublin: Stationery Office (monthly)

The *Economic Series* bulletin provides up-to-date information and five years' retrospection for a selection of 151 principal short-term economic series. Longer retrospection is given in each December issue.

Charts and graphs accompany the tables. The numbers pertaining to building and construction are as follows:

Houses completed
3.01   Total number
3.02   Local Authority
3.03   Other

Housing grants and loans
3.04   New house grants approved – number
3.05   Home improvements grants approved – number
3.06   New loans approved – number

Imports
3.08   Imports of cement

Planning permissions
3.09   Total number
3.10   Total floor area
3.11   Houses – number of units
3.12   Flats – number of units

Building costs
3.13   House Building Cost Index

Employment
3.14   Employment Index

Average weekly earnings
3.15   Skilled workers
3.16   Unskilled workers

Average hourly earnings
3.17   Skilled workers
3.18   Unskilled workers

Recommended payments for new construction
3.19   Industrial sector
3.20   Commercial sector
3.21   Health, education and other sectors

Central Statistics Office
STATISTICAL ABSTRACT
Dublin: Stationery Office (annually)

Each issue of the *Statistical Abstract* contains a section on building and construction. The tables are supported by an explanatory text. Examples from the 1996 *Statistical Abstract* are as follows.

Private sector census of building and construction
- summary of the activity of private building and construction firms with 20 or more persons engaged in 1993 and 1994

Earnings and employment
- average earnings and hours worked by skilled and unskilled operatives for private firms with 10 or more persons engaged, 1990–1995
- Monthly Employment Index for private firms with 5 or more persons engaged, 1990–1995

Number of dwellings completed
- total number of dwellings completed, 1990–1995
- number of Local Authority dwellings completed, 1990–1995
- number of non-Local Authority dwellings completed, 1990–1995

Housing grants
- number of new house grants approved, 1990–1995
- number of home improvement grants approved, 1990–1995
- number of new loans approved, 1990–1995
- public capital expenditure on housing, 1990–1995

Planning permissions

Quantity surveyors inquiry
- summary of recommended payments for new construction (non-residential), 1990–1995

Construction output
- value of construction output in current prices, 1990–1995

Cement
- imports of cement, 1990–1995

Cost index
- Monthly House Building Cost Index, 1990–1996

Central Statistics Office
STATISTICAL ABSTRACT
Dublin: Stationery Office (annually)

Each issue of the *Statistical Abstract* contains a section on housing. The tables are supported by an explanatory text. Examples from the 1996 *Statistical Abstract* are as follows.

Housing and social amenities
- permanent private housing units in 1991 in each province, county and county borough classified by period in which built – Census of Population, 1991
- persons in private households in permanent housing units and number of rooms occupied in each province, county and county borough – Census of Population, 1991
- permanent housing units in each province, county and county borough classified by nature of occupancy – Census of Population, 1991

Central Statistics Office
STATISTICAL BULLETIN + Index
Dublin: Stationery Office (quarterly)

The Census of Building and Construction is published in the *Statistical Bulletin*. The 1994 Census of Building and Construction – results for private firms with 20 or more persons engaged – was published in the *Statistical Bulletin*, December 1996.

Figures are given in the following tables.
Table 1: Summary of the activity of private building and construction firms with 20 or persons

engaged in 1993 and 1994 (number of employees, labour costs, wages and salaries turnover, purchases, stocks at end of year, stock changes, capital assets, etc.)

Table 2: Large firms – details of turnover as a principal contractor (new construction, repairs and maintenance)

Table 3: Large firms – details of purchases of materials and fuels

Table 4: Large firms – details of other costs

Table 5: Large firms – details of employment

Table 6: Large firms – details of acquisition of capital assets.

Central Statistics Office
STATISTICAL BULLETIN + Index
Dublin: Stationery Office (quarterly)

Each issue of the *Statistical Bulletin* contains data on employment, earnings and hours worked for persons employed in manufacturing industry and in building and construction. Listed below are the relevant tables for construction workers.

- average earnings and hours worked in private firms with ten or more persons engaged
- average earnings and hours worked by skilled and unskilled operatives
- average earnings and hours worked for main categories of employees
- monthly index for employment in private firms with five or more persons engaged

---

Central Statistics Office
STATISTICAL RELEASES
Dublin: Central Statistics Office

Statistical Releases issued by the Central Statistics Office update the information and statistics in the *Statistical Bulletin*. The *Releases* issued for building and construction are:

- Census of building and construction – overall results (annually)
- Average earnings and hours worked in building and construction (quarterly)
- Index of employment in building and construction (monthly)

Department of the Environment*
ANNUAL HOUSING STATISTICS BULLETIN (incorporating the December quarter)
Dublin: Stationery Office (annually)

The *Annual Housing Statistics Bulletin 1996* was published in February 1997 and comprises statistical tables in 13 principal sections as follows.

Housing activity
- aggregate house completions
- private house completions by area
- new houses completed by type

Housing loans
- loan approvals and payments (all agencies, building societies, banks and Local Authorities)
- percentage share of mortgage market

- ranges of loans paid – whole country

Profile of borrowers
- marital status of borrowers
- occupation of borrowers

House prices and costs
- new and second-hand house prices
- price/earnings/cost indices
- house building cost index

Local Authority housing

Activity under social housing schemes

Traveller families in Local Authority accommodation or on the roadside

Housing grants
- new house grants
- house improvement grants
- water and sewerage grants

Enforcement of statutory requirements – rented housing 1995

Housing (registration of rented houses) Regulations 1996

Capital investment in housing

Assessment of Local Authority housing needs

Assessment of the number of homeless persons

* Since July 1997 Department of the Environment and Local Government.

Department of the Environment*
CONSTRUCTION INDUSTRY REVIEW AND OUTLOOK (year)
Dublin: Stationery Office (annually)

This bulletin contains:

- a general review of the construction industry in Ireland
- construction output by region
- sectoral review and outlook
- employment in building and construction
- construction output by sector
- public capital expenditure in building and construction
- building and construction price index
- residential construction
- index of house prices
- medium-term review and outlook

* Since July 1997 Department of the Environment and Local Government.

Department of the Environment*
HOUSING STATISTICS BULLETIN
Dublin: Stationery Office (quarterly)

The December issue of the *Housing Statistics Bulletin* is incorporated in the *Annual Housing Statistics Bulletin*. The bulletin for each quarter contains the same type of information as that given in the *Annual Housing Statistics Bulletin*.

* Since July 1997 Department of the Environment and Local Government.

Other Publications: Irish

Construction Industry Federation (CIF)
ANNUAL REPORT
Dublin: Construction Industry Federation (annually)

The CIF has approximately 23 specialist associations. It represents its members at industrial tribunals, and represents the construction industry to the Government and other organisations on economic and financial matters.

The President and Director General's statements comment on:

- performance of the Irish economy
- economic output and employment growth
- housing demand and need for investment in construction
- urban renewal schemes and new projects
- VAT on building materials and taxation policy
- performance of the construction sector.

The Strategic Review Committee report contains about 80 recommendations for assisting the construction sector and improving efficiency and competitiveness.

The *Annual Report* also includes a review of the performance of the various sectors of the construction industry for every region in Ireland.

CRH plc (Cement Roadstone Holdings)
ANNUAL REPORT
Dublin: CRH plc (annually)

CRH plc is a leading manufacturer and supplier of building materials with headquarters in Dublin. In Ireland, CRH is the largest supplier of cement, aggregates, asphalt, readymixed concrete and concrete products. It has extensive operations in mainland Europe, Great Britain, Northern Ireland and the United States.

The Chairman's statement and the Chief Executive's review comment on:

- the performance of the Group

- sales and trading profits
- developments in the construction industry and outlook for building
- performance of Irish Cement, Roadstone-Wood Group, Premier Periclase, T.B.F., Thompson Group, etc.
- operations of other subsidiary companies.

The *Annual Report* includes the Directors' Report and the financial statements.

Housing Finance Agency plc
ANNUAL REPORT AND ACCOUNTS
Dublin: Housing Finance Agency plc (annually)

The Housing Finance Agency was established under the Housing Finance Agency Act 1981. It lends money to local authorities for Local Authority housing and also lends money to the National Building Agency.

The Chairman's Report and the Directors' Report assess:

- performance of the Agency
- lending programme
- loan advances to local authorities
- profitability of the Agency.

Publications: International Organisations

United Nations. Economic Commission for Europe (ECE)
ANNUAL BULLETIN OF HOUSING AND BUILDING STATISTICS FOR EUROPE
New York: United Nations (annually)

This bulletin comprises statistical tables on housing and building in European countries, Canada and the United States. It gives data on the following:

Building materials
Production, imports/exports, consumption of cement, production of building materials

Dwelling construction
Dwelling stock and new dwellings completed

General statistics
Estimates of population and rate of change, gross fixed capital formation

Labour
Indices of employment and unemployment

Price indices
Wholesale price indices of building materials, consumer price indices, rent indices, input~output price indices for housing construction

Annex
- list of the Commission's reports in housing and building
- sources of data and general notes

Industry: Industrial Organisation

Official Publications

Department of Enterprise and Employment*
ANNUAL REPORT
Dublin: Stationery Office (annually)

The *Annual Report* contains:

- a review by the Secretary of the Department in which he comments on the mission, objectives and performance of the Department, such as: measures to combat unemployment, employment creation policies, economic and industrial development strategies
- organisation and structure of the Department
- enterprise programmes and strategies
- performance of Forfás (the agency which provides policy advice to the Minister and the Department on a broad range of issues affecting industrial development in Ireland)
- performance of IDA Ireland (established in 1994, the task of IDA Ireland is to bring new business to Ireland and to promote the expansion of the existing base of overseas companies)
- performance of Forbairt (established in 1994, Forbairt's task is to provide support and services to indigenous industry)
- Ireland's science and technology policy and programmes
- European Union Structural Funds and Ireland's Operational Programme for Industrial Development 1994–1999
- list of Statutory Instruments made during the year under review
- redundancies notified within each industrial sector
- matters relating to industrial relations, labour law, occupational safety, etc.

* Since July 1997 Department of Enterprise, Trade and Employment.

Other Publications: Irish

Forbairt*
ANNUAL REPORT AND ACCOUNTS
Dublin: Forbairt (annually)

Forbairt was established in accordance with the Industrial Development Act 1993. Its main objectives are:

- to upgrade the performance of Irish industry
- to increase employment
- to improve profitability in indigenous enterprises
- to fund schemes which support R&D
- to fund investment in technology and innovation.

The Chairman's Statement and the Chief Executive's Report comment on:

- the performance of Irish industry
- performance of specific sectors (computer industry, food industry, clothing industry, etc.)

- support services for Irish businesses
- investment in enterprises, projects and companies
- technology and innovation in industry
- competitiveness of indigenous industry.

The *Annual Report* also includes the financial statements and organisation and structure of the Board.

* Since July 1998 the functions of Forbairt have been absorbed by Enterprise Ireland.

Forbairt
ANNUAL REVIEW
Dublin: Forbairt (annually)

Forbairt was established in 1993 and published its first *Annual Review* (for 1994) in 1995. The second *Annual Review* was published in 1996. It contains:

- an overall assessment of the performance of Irish industry
- detailed reports of developments in science and innovation, food sector, information technology, business development, manufacturing industry, clothing and textile sector, print sector, furniture sector, agri-business, forestry, etc.
- investment in various programmes and schemes
- Forbairt's mission statement
- organisation and structure of the Board.

Forfás - the Policy and Advisory Board for Industrial Development and Science & Technology in Ireland
ANNUAL REPORT AND ACCOUNTS
Dublin: Forfás (annually)

Forfás was established pursuant to the Industrial Development Act 1993 and is the policy and advisory co-ordination board for industrial development and science & technology in Ireland. It is also the body through which powers are delegated to Forbairt for the promotion of indigenous industry and to IDA Ireland for the promotion of inward investment. The broad functions of Forfás are to:

- advise the Minister on matters relating to the development of industry in Ireland
- advise on the development and co-ordination of policy for Forbairt, IDA Ireland, An Bord Tráchtála and other such bodies as the Minister may designate
- promote science and technology for economic and social development
- encourage the establishment and development in the State of foreign industrial undertakings
- advise and co-ordinate Forbairt and IDA Ireland in relation to their functions.

The Chairman's Statement and the Chief Executive's Report comment on:

- performance of the Irish economy and economic achievement
- competitiveness of Irish industry
- innovation
- development and skills of the workforce
- investment in science and technology
- investment in industry

- employment creation
- performance of Irish-owned enterprises and foreign-owned enterprises.

Text, tables, graphs and charts cover:
- developments in the major world economies
- performance of manufacturing industry
- R&D in the business sector
- employment growth
- employment in manufacturing and international services
- international trends in manufacturing employment
- corporate tax – Forfás conducts an annual survey of corporation tax payments by companies in the manufacturing and internationally traded services sectors
- energy policy
- regional policy
- environmental policy.

The *Annual Report* also includes the organisation and structure of the Board.

IBEC – Irish Business and Employers Confederation
ANNUAL REVIEW
Dublin: IBEC (annually)

In the *Annual Review* the President of IBEC comments on:

- performance of the Irish economy and Irish business
- job creation, employment and unemployment
- impact of the Budget on business
- European issues such as the European Monetary Union (EMU), Cohesion Funds and Structural Funds.

The review also contains further information on:

- growth and performance of the Irish economy
- consumer demand and expenditure
- taxation
- competitiveness of Irish manufacturing industry
- performance of the specific sectors, i.e. manufacturing industry, services sector, energy sector, transport, telecommunications, agri-business, fishing industry, building and construction, food, drink and tobacco sector.

IBEC – Irish Business and Employers Confederation
ECONOMIC TRENDS
Dublin: IBEC (monthly)

Economic Trends gives a brief review of developments in the Irish economy, such as:

- the move towards European Monetary Union (EMU)
- the Budget – an analysis
- business and investment

Each issue contains charts and graphs accompanied by an explanatory text on:

- manufacturing output
- order books
- production expectations
- capacity utilisation
- live register
- wholesale prices
- output prices
- consumer prices
- retail sales
- construction employment
- building employment index
- volume of imports
- volume of exports
- exchange rates.

IBEC – Irish Business and Employers Confederation
ECONOMIC TRENDS – QUARTERLY REVIEW
Dublin: IBEC (quarterly)

This covers various aspects of the Irish economy. The text is accompanied by charts and graphs, and topics covered include:

- the labour force – employment and unemployment in the different sectors of the economy
- manufacturing output, capacity utilisation, order books
- consumer spending
- retail sales
- Government spending
- investment in plant and machinery, construction and building, etc.
- balance of payments
- external trade
- exchange rates and interest rates
- international outlook
- European Commission forecast of the Irish economy
- production expectations
- output prices
- consumer price index
- inflation figures for European Union countries
- taxation
- social welfare
- summary of the most recent Budget
- taxation measures.

IBEC – Irish Business and Employers Confederation
IBEC NEWS
Dublin: IBEC (monthly)

IBEC News gives a brief review of current developments in industry. Topics covered include:

- working time
- trade policy
- roads
- telecommunications
- exchange rates and inflation
- the euro: update of changeover plan
- competition policy
- taxation policy
- unemployment
- strikes and industrial disputes.

IBEC – Irish Business and Employers Confederation
IBEC/ESRI MONTHLY INDUSTRIAL SURVEY
Dublin: IBEC (monthly)

The *Monthly Industrial Survey* is carried out by the Irish Business and Employers Confederation (IBEC) and the Economic and Social Research Institute (ESRI) using a statistically representative sample of manufacturing firms in Ireland.

Industries have been grouped together in three broad categories, i.e. consumer goods, capital goods and intermediate groups. The text is supported by charts and graphs, and information is given on:

- production – assessment and expectations
- home sales – assessment and expectations
- exports – assessment and expectations
- employment – expectations
- order books – current situation and new orders
- stocks of raw materials and stocks of finished products
- capacity utilisation and adequacy of capacity for the next year
- selling prices – trends.

IDA Ireland (Industrial Development Agency)
ANNUAL REPORT
Dublin: IDA Ireland (annually)

The Industrial Development Agency (Ireland) was established pursuant to the Industrial Development Act 1993. Its main objectives are:

- to attract overseas companies to Ireland
- to win new investment projects
- to create employment
- to assist in industrial development.

The Chairman's Statement and the Chief Executive's Report comment on:

- performance of IDA Ireland
- competitiveness of Irish industry
- job creation
- performance of overseas companies
- growth in manufacturing industry
- growth in the services sector

- regional development
- figures for new jobs by region
- figures for total employment by region.

The *Annual Report* also includes the financial statements and the organisation and structure of the Board.

Publications: International Organisations

European Communities, Eurostat (Statistical Office of the EC)
MONTHLY PANORAMA OF EUROPEAN INDUSTRY
Luxembourg: Office for Official Publications of the European Communities (monthly)

At the beginning of 1997 *Industrial Trends – Monthly Statistics* merged with *Monthly Panorama of European Industry*, which sets out to present a summary picture of manufacturing industry in the European Union. Issues comprise text, charts, graphs, maps and tables, and cover topics such as:

- competitiveness of manufacturing industry in the EU Member States
- production
- employment
- labour productivity
- wages
- performance and competitiveness of various industrial sectors (chemicals; metal products; transport equipment; food; drink and tobacco; computers and electrical appliances; etc.)
- latest developments in the European economy in comparison with Japan and the USA
- business cycles at a glance
- regional analysis
- export share competitiveness analysis.

Certain issues contain 'special articles' such as:
- recent trends in the steel industry
- the construction industry
- structure of European industry
- competitiveness.

European Communities, Eurostat (Statistical Office of the EC)
PANORAMA OF EU INDUSTRY (Volumes 1 and 2)
Luxembourg: Office for Official Publications of the European Communities (annually + six short-term supplements)

Panorama of EU Industry gives an extensive review of the situation and outlook for the manufacturing and service industries in the European Union. The 1997 edition presents the recent trends and outlook for approximately 200 manufacturing and services sectors in the EU.

Charts, graphs and tables accompany the sections summarised below.

Special features
- highlights of EU industry
- the impact and effectiveness of the Single Market
- the world's largest industrial groups

- European competitiveness
- outlook for employment by sector
- analysis of growth markets

Reviews and forecasts: industrial sectors
Overview and analysis of the following sectors:

- energy
- non-energy: mining and quarrying
- food, drink and tobacco
- textiles, clothing, leather and footwear
- wood processing
- pulp, paper, printing and publishing
- chemicals
- rubber and plastics
- non-metallic mineral products
- ferrous metals
- instrument engineering
- transport equipment
- construction.

The analysis includes a profile of the sector, recent trends, international comparisons, demand, supply and competition, structure of the industry, regional distribution, regulations, policies and outlook.

Reviews and forecasts: service sectors
- distribution (wholesale trade, retail trade)
- tourism (restaurants, hotels, accommodation, recreation parks, travel services)
- transport services (railway transport, public transport, road passenger transport, road freight transport, inland waterways, shipping, air transport, etc.)
- financial services (financial institutions, credit institutions, banks, insurance companies, etc.)
- business services (advertising, marketing, public relations, legal services, accountancy services, management consultancy, engineering, architects, linguistic services, franchising, etc.)
- information services
- audiovisual services

European Communities, Eurostat (Statistical Office of the EC)
PANORAMA OF EU INDUSTRY: short-term supplements
Luxembourg: Office for Official Publications of the European Communities (bimonthly)

These supplements contain statistics, comments and graphs on recent trends in European industry. The first part deals with overall trends and the situation in the intermediate goods, capital goods and consumer goods sector. The second part looks at two specific industries in detail. The aim is to cover the major industries once a year.

European Communities, Eurostat (Statistical Office of the EC)
THE STRUCTURAL FUNDS IN (year)
Luxembourg: Office for Official Publications of the European Communities (annually)

The Structural Funds in 1995, published in 1996, is the seventh annual report. It contains information on matters such as:

- integration of the new Member States into the EU structural policies
- launch of Community Initiative programmes
- employment and job creation measures
- EU assistance by objectives
- Community Initiatives
- implementation of the EU Budget
- implementation of the Structural Funds
- regional development Initiatives
- rural development Initiative (LEADER Programme)
- urban development Initiatives.

European Communities, Eurostat (Statistical Office of the EC)
STRUCTURE AND ACTIVITY OF INDUSTRY – Annual Inquiry – Main Results
Luxembourg: Office for Official Publications of the European Communities (every four years)

Coverage includes the EU Member States and EFTA countries. It gives an overview of annual industrial employment, investment, operating income and expenditure and production levels, how these levels change, which sectors are dominant for each of the production factors, how high costs are, how efficient the production process is, how enterprises of different sizes contribute to employment and output, how production and investment are spread over different regions, etc.

Organisation for Economic Co-operation and Development (OECD)
INDUSTRIAL STRUCTURE STATISTICS
Paris: OECD (annually)

Industrial Structure Statistics 1994 was published in 1996 and comprises four sections.

Section 1: Industrial survey and foreign trade statistics
Industries are coded and grouped according to the International Standard Industrial Classification (ISIC). For each country figures are given for production, value added, employment, investment in machinery and equipment, wages and salaries, number of establishments, etc.

Section 2: Disaggregated national accounts by industry

Section 3: Currency abbreviations

Section 4: Definitions of the International Standard Industrial Classification (ISIC)

Industry: Industrial Production

Central Statistics Office
CENSUS OF INDUSTRIAL PRODUCTION
Dublin: Stationery Office (annually)

The *Census of Industrial Production 1994* was taken in accordance with SI 81/1993 and was published in June 1997. It is set out in three parts as follows.

Part 1 – Description of the Census

Part 2 – Results of the 1994 Census of Industrial Local Units (with three or more persons engaged)

Industrial local units 1994
- details of activity (59 variables) for each industrial sector
- details of activity (59 variables) in each county and regional authority
- summary of activity (11 variables) in broad industrial sectors classified by number of persons engaged
- summary of activity (11 variables) in each regional authority classified by number of persons engaged

Manufacturing local units 1994
- components of change in the number of local units and persons engaged between 1993 and 1994 classified by major manufacturing sector, nationality of ownership and IDA Ireland/Forbairt grant status
- summary of activity (11 variables) in broad industrial sectors classified by nationality of ownership
- summary of activity (11 variables) in broad industrial sectors classified by IDA Ireland/Forbairt grant type
- summary of activity (11 variables) for all local units classified by nationality of ownership and IDA Ireland/Forbairt grant type
- gross output, percentage of imported materials and exports classified by major industrial sector and nationality of ownership
- gross output, percentage of imported materials and exports classified by broad industrial sector
- gross output, percentage of imported materials and exports classified by nationality of ownership and number of persons engaged

Industrial local units 1994
- number of local units in broad industrial sectors classified by:
  - number of persons engaged per local unit
  - county and regional authority
  - gross output per local unit
  - net output per local unit
  - net output per person engaged
- number of local units in major industrial sectors classified by:
  - persons engaged and net output per person engaged
  - persons engaged and wages and salaries per employee.

Part 3 – Results of the 1994 Census of Industrial Enterprises (with three or more persons engaged)
Industrial enterprises 1994
- details of activity in broad industrial sectors
- details of activity in all industrial sectors classified by number of persons engaged per enterprise
- details of activity in all industrial sectors classified by turnover per enterprise

NACE codes and corresponding industrial sectors are contained in Appendix 1.

Central Statistics Office
ECONOMIC SERIES
Dublin: Stationery Office (monthly)

The *Economic Series* bulletin provides up-to-date information and five years' retrospection for a selection of 151 principal short-term economic series. Longer retrospection is given in each December issue.

Charts and graphs accompany the tables. The numbers pertaining to industrial production are as follows.

Industrial Production Index
2.01	All industry
2.02	All industry (seasonally adjusted)
2.03	Manufacturing industry
2.04	Manufacturing industry (seasonally adjusted)
2.05	Electricity generating stations output

Industrial Turnover Index
2.06	Manufacturing industry
2.07	Manufacturing industry (seasonally adjusted)

Central Statistics Office
STATISTICAL ABSTRACT
Dublin: Stationery Office (annually)

Each issue of the *Statistical Abstract* contains a section on industrial production. The tables are supported by an explanatory text. Examples from the 1996 *Statistical Abstract* are listed below.

Industrial production
- industrial establishments – main variables for all industries (NACE 1–4), 1973–1990
- industrial local units: gross output, net output, wages and salaries and persons engaged in each industrial sector, 1991–1993
- industrial enterprises: number of enterprises, employment, turnover, purchases, gross value added, labour costs, stocks, acquisitions of capital assets for the main industrial sectors, 1991–1993

Industrial Production Index
- monthly volume of production indices for manufacturing, transportable goods and all industries, 1991–1995

- monthly volume of production indices for major industrial groups (unadjusted), 1991–1995
- monthly volume of production indices for major industrial groups (seasonally adjusted), 1991–1995

Industrial Turnover Index – monthly
- industrial turnover indices for manufacturing and transportable goods industries, 1991–1995
- monthly industrial turnover indices for major industrial groups (unadjusted), 1991–1995
- monthly industrial turnover indices for major industrial groups (seasonally adjusted), 1991–1995

Central Statistics Office
STATISTICAL BULLETIN + Index
Dublin: Stationery Office (quarterly)

The Industrial Production Index monitors current trends in the volume of production of industrial establishments with three or more persons engaged.

Figures for a four-year period are published in the following tables in each issue of the *Statistical Bulletin.*

- *Table 1:* Volume of production indices for manufacturing, transportable goods and all industries (Base: year 1985 = 100)
- *Table 2:* Monthly volume of production indices for manufacturing, transportable goods and all industries
- *Table 3:* Monthly, quarterly and annual volume of production indices for industrial sectors – unadjusted
- *Table 4:* Monthly and quarterly volume of production indices for industrial sectors – seasonally adjusted

The Industrial Turnover Index complements the Industrial Production Index, which monitors trends in the volume of production.

Turnover indices are provided in the tables listed below.

- *Table 1:* Annual and quarterly turnover indices for manufacturing and transportable goods industries
- *Table 2:* Monthly turnover indices for manufacturing and transportable goods industries
- *Table 3:* Monthly, quarterly and annual turnover indices for industrial sectors – unadjusted
- *Table 4:* Monthly and quarterly turnover indices for industrial sectors – seasonally adjusted

Base: year 1980 = 100. Industries have been arranged according to the NACE code.

Department of Finance
ECONOMIC REVIEW AND OUTLOOK
Dublin: Stationery Office (annually)

The appendix in the *Economic Review and Outlook* comprises statistical tables with comparative figures for approximately nine years. The table relevant to production is encaptioned

'Volume of production indices in major industrial sectors'.

Department of Foreign Affairs
DEVELOPMENTS IN THE EUROPEAN UNION
Dublin: Stationery Office (biannually)

In accordance with Section 5 of the 1972 European Communities Act, the Government is required to submit twice yearly to each House of the Oireachtas a report on the developments in the European Communities. Topics relevant to industrial policy include:

- EU directives and regulations
- industrial competitiveness
- financial activities of the European Coal and Steel Community
- restructuring of the steel industry
- developments in copyright protection
- developments in the electronic industry, pharmaceutical industry, public procurement.

Other Publications: Irish

National Competitiveness Council
ANNUAL COMPETITIVENESS REPORT
Dublin: Forfás (annually)

The National Competitiveness Council was established in May 1997 as a part of the Partnership 2000 agreement. The Council's terms of reference require it to report to the Taoiseach on key competitiveness issues, with recommendations on policy actions required to improve Ireland's competitive position.

The *Annual Competitiveness Report 1998* gives an overview of the work of the Council and the Irish economy and contains information on:

- competitiveness (the global situation, Ireland's main competitors, EMU, costs, international comparisons, competitiveness of the Irish economy)
- human resources development (education and training, labour markets, labour costs and productivity, work incentives, employment)
- business services (technological innovation and performance)
- international trade
- finance (financial markets, investment)
- infrastructure (telecommunications quality and costs)
- transport
- energy
- planning, property and construction (planning process and construction costs)
- SME – small and medium-sized enterprises, performance
- public administration (State intervention for the smooth running of markets, strategic planning, prevention of market distortions, quality of service provided by the public and private sectors).

National Competitiveness Council – other publications

- *Ireland's Costs and Competitiveness Environment*, 1995
- *Competitiveness Challenge: Council Summary Statement*, 1998

Publications: International Organisations

European Communities, Eurostat (Statistical Office of the EC)
INDUSTRIAL TRENDS – monthly statistics
Luxembourg: Office for Official Publications of the European Communities (monthly)

This bulletin provides monthly information on short-term trends in industry in the European Union. It comprises statistical tables grouped in the sections summarised below.

Basic indicators
- production indices
- price indices

Data by industry
- capital goods industries
- durable consumer goods industries
- non-durable consumer goods industries
- manufacturing industry

Graphs for selected industries
- food, drink and tobacco industry
- clothing industry
- footwear and leather industry
- paper industry
- chemical industry
- manufacturing industry (various items)
- electricity, gas, steam and hot water supply

Construction and building
- indices of production
- number of employees

European Communities, Eurostat (Statistical Office of the EC)
IRON AND STEEL – monthly
Luxembourg: Office for Official Publications of the European Communities (monthly)

This bulletin comprises statistical tables which give figures for:

- the ECSC steel situation
- pig iron production
- crude steel production
- long products and heavy sections – total
- flat products – total
- hot rolled plates and sheets
- new orders for non-alloy steels

- production and deliveries of alloy and non-alloy steels
- imports of ECSC steel from third countries
- exports of ECSC steel to third countries
- imports of ECSC steel products from third countries
- exports of ECSC steel products to third countries
- consumption of scrap by the iron and steel industry
- total labour force
- hours worked
- total working hours lost.

European Communities, Eurostat (Statistical Office of the EC)
IRON AND STEEL – yearly statistics
Luxembourg: Office for Official Publications of the European Communities (annually)

The *Iron and Steel* yearbook comprises statistical tables grouped in the sections summarised below.

Main summary tables
- population and Gross Domestic Product
- indices of industrial production (EU)
- crude steel balances (EU)
- results of the Annual Inquiry into Industrial Activity

Production bases
- employees in the iron and steel industry (situation at end of year)
- employees in industry (yearly average)
- production and stocks of iron ore
- consumption of pig iron, spiegel and high carbon ferromanganese (by Member States)
- consumption and deliveries of power in the iron and steel industry (EU)

Production
- production ratios
- world pig iron production
- pig iron production by Member States
- world crude steel production
- the 30 most important crude steel producers in the world

Works deliveries
- works deliveries of steel (EU)

Foreign trade

Steel consumption

Investment

Prices, average values, wages

Levy
- levy rate
- share of contribution of each country to the ECSC levy

Organisation for Economic Co-operation and Development (OECD)
INDICATORS OF INDUSTRIAL ACTIVITY
Paris: OECD (quarterly)

This provides an overall view of short-term economic developments in different industries for all OECD member countries. It comprises two sections.

Section 1 – quantitative indicators
Indices for industrial production, mining and quarrying, manufacturing industry (main branches), chemicals, non-metallic mineral products, base metals, metal products, machinery and equipment, electricity, gas and water.

Section 2 – qualitative indicators
Data in this section are derived from business surveys carried out in OECD countries. Tables contain indices for stocks of finished goods, state of order books, production prospects, rate of capacity utilisation, labour force expectations, total order inflows.

Organisation for Economic Co-operation and Development (OECD)
PULP AND PAPER INDUSTRY
Paris: OECD (annually)

This comprises statistical tables which contain figures for:

- wood pulp production
- paper and paperboard production
- comparison between industrial production and production of pulp and paper in a given period
- production and consumption of woodpulp
- production and consumption of paper and board
- production capacity utilisation
- production capacity of woodpulp, paper and board.

United Nations. Department for Economic and Social Information and Policy Analysis
INDUSTRIAL COMMODITY STATISTICS YEARBOOK: production and consumption statistics
New York: United Nations (annually)

The *Industrial Commodity Statistics Yearbook 1994* was published in 1994. It comprises statistical tables arranged in two parts.

Part 1: Commodity production (ten-year period)
Contains data on production of industrial commodities by country, and geographical region for the world.

Mining and quarrying (coal, crude petroleum, ferrous and non-ferrous metal ores, non-metallic minerals and fertilisers)

Manufacturing (food, beverages, tobacco, textiles, wearing apparel, leather and leather products, paper and paper products, rubber products, products of petroleum and coal, transport equipment, etc.)

Electricity and gas (electricity, gas produced by works)

Part 2: Consumption of selected commodities
Contains data by country on the consumption of about 200 industrial commodities.

United Nations. Department for Economic and Social Information and Policy Analysis
STATISTICAL YEARBOOK
New York: United Nations (annually)

The *Statistical Yearbook* is international in scope. Countries are listed in alphabetical order. Figures for industrial production are contained in the following tables.

- manufacturing industries: production and consumption
- food, beverages and tobacco
- textiles, wearing apparel
- leather industries and footwear
- paper and paper products
- machinery and equipment

United Nations. Economic Commission for Europe (ECE)
ANNUAL BULLETIN OF STEEL STATISTICS FOR EUROPE AND NORTH AMERICA
Geneva: United Nations (annually)

This comprises statistical tables preceded by explanatory notes. Examples are listed below.

Summary tables
- production of raw materials and iron products
- production of steel products
- steel industry deliveries and receipts
- imports and exports of raw materials and iron and steel products
- consumption of raw materials in the steel industry
- movements of iron and steel scrap
- consumption of energy in the steel industry

Country tables
- imports and exports of raw materials
- imports and exports of iron and steel products

United Nations. Economic Commission for Europe (ECE)
THE CHEMICAL INDUSTRY – ANNUAL REVIEW
New York: United Nations (annually)

This comprises, text, charts and tables grouped in two parts.

Part 1: General review of the chemical industry
- general developments in the chemical industry
- global economic situation
- the chemical industry in developed market economies (Western Europe, North America, Japan)

- the chemical industry in transition economies
- developments in selected sectors of the chemical industry (petrochemicals and plastics, man-made fibres, chlorine/caustic soda, fertilisers)
- list of mergers, acquisitions and joint ventures in the current year

Part 2: Statistical tables
- general industrial and trade statistics in the chemical industry for previous years
- production, imports and exports of selected chemical products for previous years
- imports and exports of chemical products by SITC groups
- origin of imports and destination of exports for selected countries
- list of recent publications of the Chemical Industry Section of the UN/ECE Industry and Technology Division

United Nations. Economic Commission for Europe (ECE)
ANNUAL REVIEW OF ENGINEERING INDUSTRIES AND AUTOMATION
New York: United Nations (annually)

This comprises text supported by tables, and has data on the following.

International economic developments, particularly as regards the engineering industries, e.g.

- per capita gross production and value added for engineering industries (selected countries)
- price indices of the engineering industries
- export price index of machinery and transport equipment
- price indices for exports of machinery and transport equipment by major developed market-economy countries
- gross fixed capital formation in the engineering industries
- production of metal goods and machine-cutting metal tools
- growth of the computer industry
- production of electrical machinery and power transformers
- production of transport equipment
- merchant ships completed, by region
- estimated consumption by end-use market in the United States and Western Europe
- world exports of engineering products
- share of exports of engineering products of the total exports of selected regions and countries
- balance of international trade in all metal and engineering products
- exports of metal and engineering products of selected countries, by groups of product
- total exports of engineering products of main exporters by destination

Developments in specific countries

United Nations. Economic Commission for Europe (ECE)
THE STEEL MARKET IN (year)
New York: United Nations (annually)

The bulletin comprises text supported by tables. Coverage includes European countries, Canada, United States and the former USSR.

Part 1
- review of and outlook for the steel market
- international developments in:
  - trends in steel demand, supply and prices
  - trends in demand for and prices of iron and steel making
    raw materials

Part 2
- country data
  - trends in iron and steel production
  - foreign trade in steel
  - trends in demand, by principal sectors
  - output of principal steel-using sectors
  - steel deliveries by producers (by main sectors and by main product)
  - employment in the iron and steel industry
  - investment expenditure, by production stages
  - trends in domestic base prices
  - existing capacity

Labour

Official Publications

Central Statistics Office
ECONOMIC SERIES
Dublin: Stationery Office (monthly)

The *Economic Series* bulletin provides up-to-date information and five years' retrospection for a selection of 151 principal short-term economic series. Longer retrospection is given in each December issue.

Charts and graphs accompany the tables. Listed below are the numbers pertaining to employment, earnings and productivity in manufacturing industry.

Employment
2.08   Manufacturing industry
2.09   Manufacturing industry (seasonally adjusted)

Earnings – manufacturing industry
Average weekly earnings
2.10   Adult males
2.11   Adult females
2.12   All industrial workers

Average hourly earnings
2.13   Adult males
2.14   Adult females
2.15   All industrial workers

Productivity – manufacturing industry
2.16   Unit wage costs – manufacturing industry
2.17   Output per person
2.18   Output per hour

Listed below are the numbers pertaining to the services sector.

Total persons engaged
7.01   Banking, insurance and building societies
7.02   Banking
7.03   Insurance
7.04   Building societies

Index of weekly earnings for all employees
7.05   Banking, insurance and building societies
7.06   Banking
7.07   Insurance
7.08   Building societies

Listed below are the numbers pertaining to unemployment.

Live Register
9.01   Total persons
9.02   Males
9.03   Females
9.04   Total (SA)
9.05   Males (SA)
9.06   Females (SA)

Live Register – persons under 25 years
9.07   Total
9.08   Total (SA)
9.09   Seasonally adjusted standardised unemployment rates

Average flows
9.10   Onto Live Register
9.11   Off Live Register

Redundancies
9.14   Redundancies notified under the Redundancy Payments Act

---

Central Statistics Office
LABOUR COSTS SURVEY
Dublin: Central Statistics Office (periodically)

Labour Costs Surveys have been undertaken for the distribution, credit and insurance sectors in 1974, for the industrial sector in 1975 and for all four of these sectors in respect of 1978, 1981, 1984, 1988 and 1992 in compliance with EU Regulations. Coverage was extended to include the business services sector and travel agents for the 1992 survey which was initiated in the second half of 1993. These surveys provide detailed estimates of labour costs (i.e. wages and salaries, social security payments, training costs, redundancy payments, etc.) of enterprises classified by activity and size.

The *Labour Costs Survey, 1992* in industry, distribution, credit, insurance and business services was published in 1995. It is divided into two parts. Examples of the tables are listed below.

Part 1: Labour costs of enterprises with ten or more employees classified by NACE 70 activity

- total labour costs of all employees
- percentage distribution of labour costs
- employment, average hours worked and average labour costs per employee in enterprises with ten or more employees
- employment, average hours worked and average labour costs per employee in enterprises with 10–49 employees, 50–99 employees, 100–199 employees, 200 or more employees

Part 2: Labour costs of enterprises with ten or more employees classified by NACE Rev. 1 activity

- total labour costs of all employees
- percentage distribution of labour costs
- employment, average hours worked and average labour costs per employee in

enterprises with ten or more employees
- employment, average hours worked and average labour costs per employee in enterprises with 10–49 employees, 50–99 employees, 100–199 employees, 200 or more employees

Central Statistics Office
LABOUR FORCE SURVEY
Dublin: Central Statistics Office (annually to 1997)

The *Labour Force Survey* is the definitive source of data on employment and unemployment. Surveys were undertaken on a harmonised EU-wide basis in 1975, 1977, 1979 and annually from 1983. A sample of about 45,000 households was surveyed on each occasion. A quarterly survey was introduced in September 1997, and replaced the *Labour Force Survey*.

The *Labour Force Survey 1996* is divided into four parts. Listed below are examples of tables in each part.

Part 1: Population estimates
- estimated population classified by age and sex, 1989–1996
- estimated population classified by age and sex, 1996
- estimated population aged 15 years and over classified by sex, marital status and Regional Authority, 1996

Part 2: Labour force estimates based on principal economic status
- population aged 15 years and over classified by principal economic status and sex, 1991– 1996
- estimated population aged 15 years and over, classified by principal economic status, age and sex, 1996
- estimated population aged 15 years and over, classified by principal economic status and Regional Authority, 1996
- estimates of labour force, those not in the labour force and labour participation rates classified by marital status and age – males/females, 1996
- estimated persons at work classified by occupation, sex and usual hours of work, 1996
- estimated persons at work and unemployed (excluding first job seekers) classified by occupation and sex, 1996

Part 3: Labour force analysis on ILO basis
- population aged 15 years and over classified by ILO economic status in week before the survey, 1991–1996
- population aged 15 years and over classified by ILO economic status in week before the survey and by Regional Authority, 1996
- persons in employment in week before the survey, classified by type of job, sex and economic sector, 1996
- persons unemployed (ILO basis) classified by sex, age group and duration of unemployment

Part 4: Estimates of private households and family units
- estimated private households classified by Regional Authority and size of household, 1996
- estimated private households classified by number of persons at work and number of persons unemployed (including persons seeking their first regular job) in the household, 1996

- persons in the labour force in private households classified by principal economic status, sex and status in the family unit, 1996

The Labour Force Survey 1997 was published in 1997 and contains similar information to that given in the Labour Force Survey 1996.

Central Statistics Office
QUARTERLY NATIONAL HOUSEHOLD SURVEY
Dublin: Stationery Office (quarterly)

The *Quarterly National Household Survey* began in September 1997. It replaced the annual *Labour Force Survey* and provides quarterly data on employment and unemployment as well as dealing with a range of important social topics.

Listed below are the principal tables which accompany the text.

Table 1: Persons aged 15 years and over classified by ILO economic status:
- males/females/total persons aged 15 or over:
  - in labour force
  - not in labour force
- unemployment rate (%)
- participation rate (%)

Table 2: Persons in employment classified by NACE economic sector

Table 3: Labour force participation rates classified by age group and marital status

Table 4: Unemployment rates classified by sex and age group

Table 5: Persons aged 15 years and over classified by age group and duration of unemployment

Table 6: Unemployment rate and long-term unemployment rate

Table 7: Persons aged 15 years and over classified by detailed ILO economic status

Table 8: Indicators of potential labour supply

Table 9: Population aged 15 years and over classified by principal economic status

Table 10: Persons aged 15 years and over classified by ILO economic status and by principal economic status (in a particular quarter)

Central Statistics Office
STATISTICAL ABSTRACT
Dublin: Stationery Office (annually)

Each issue of the *Statistical Abstract* contains a section on industrial employment and earnings. The tables are supported by an explanatory text. Examples from the 1996 *Statistical Abstract* are listed below.

Industrial employment
- summary of total employment in manufacturing and all industries (NACE 1–4), 1989–1995
- total number of persons engaged classified by industrial sector, 1990–1995

Industrial earnings
- gross earnings and hours worked for all industrial workers (adult and non-adult rates of pay), 1990–1995
- average weekly earnings of male and female industrial workers classified by sector, 1994 and 1995
- average weekly earnings of industrial workers classified by sector, 1992–1995
- indices of productivity and unit wage costs in manufacturing industries, 1989–1995

Each issue of *Statistical Abstract* contains a section on industrial disputes. The tables are supported by an explanatory text. Examples from the 1996 *Statistical Abstract* are listed below.

FÁS and industrial disputes
- number of vacancies notified at and filled through FÁS Service Offices, 1990–1995
- particulars of industrial disputes involving stoppages of work, 1993–1995

Each issue of the *Statistical Abstract* contains a section on the Live Register (unemployment statistics). Examples from the 1996 *Statistical Abstract* are listed below.

- number of persons on Live Register on the last Friday of each month, 1991–1995
- numbers on Live Register at end of month, classified by type of claim
- number of persons under 25 years of age on Live Register at end of month, classified by type of claim, 1992–1995
- seasonally adjusted standardised unemployment rates, 1991–1995
- number of persons on the Live Register at the end of each month in each Regional Authority, 1992–1995
- number of persons on Live Register, classified by sex and age group, 1991–1995
- number of persons on Live Register, classified by duration of continuous registration, 1991–1995
- percentage distribution of the Live Register by duration of continuous registration, 1991–1995

Each issue of the *Statistical Abstract* contains a section on redundancies. In the 1996 *Statistical Abstract*, this includes the following table.

- number of proposed qualified redundancies notified to the Department of Enterprise and Employment, classified by sex and industrial group, 1994–1995.

Central Statistics Office
STATISTICAL BULLETIN + Index
Dublin: Stationery Office (quarterly)

Each issue of the *Statistical Bulletin* contains data on employment, earnings and hours worked for persons in manufacturing industry and in building and construction. Listed below are the relevant tables.

Industrial employment

- total number of persons engaged in manufacturing industries, transportable goods industries, all industries
- total number of persons engaged by industrial sector
- total number of persons engaged in 20 supplementary industrial sub-sectors

Industrial earnings and hours worked

- gross earnings and hours worked for all industrial workers
- gross earnings and hours worked for male industrial workers
- gross earnings and hours worked for female industrial workers
- gross weekly earnings of clerical, managerial and total non-industrial employees
- gross earnings and hours worked for all industrial workers
- gross earnings and hours worked for male and female industrial workers by sector
- gross weekly earnings of managerial, clerical, total non-industrial and all employees in broad industrial sectors

Building and construction

- average earnings and hours worked for private firms with ten or more persons engaged
- average earnings and hours worked by skilled and unskilled operatives
- average earnings and hours worked for main categories of employees
- monthly index of employment in private firms with five or more persons engaged

Public sector employment

The sectors covered are:
- civil service
- defence forces
- Garda Síochána
- Local Authorities
- education (excluding private institutions)
- semi-State bodies (excluding their subsidiary companies)

Public sector average earnings index

Banking, insurance and building societies

- total persons engaged in banking, insurance and building societies
- index of gross weekly earnings for all employees in banking, insurance and building societies

Unemployment statistics are published in the 'Live Register' section in each issue of the *Statistical Bulletin*. Explanatory notes accompany the tables listed below.

- number of persons on the Live Register at local employment offices at the end of each month (3 year period)
- seasonally adjusted Live Register series: total persons
- seasonally adjusted Live Register series: persons under 25 years
- number of persons working on systematic short-term basis registered at local employment offices excluded from the Live Register
- number of smallholders and self-employed persons applying for unemployment assistance and other registrants excluded from the Live Register
- number of males/females on the Live Register by planning region
- number of males/females on the Live Register by Regional Authority
- number of males on the Live Register at each local employment office

- number of females on the Live Register at each local employment office
- persons on the Live Register classified by age group each April and October
- number of persons on the Live Register on 20 October 1995 classified by sex, age and duration of continuous registration
- summary of flows on and off the Live Register and average weekly flow January to December
- summary of flows on and off the Live Register in each region in July, August and September

The June issue of the *Statistical Bulletin* has information on industrial disputes. The principal tables are:

Table 1: Disputes in progress during (year)
Table 2: Disputes classified by cause
Table 3: Disputes classified by industrial groups
Table 4: Disputes classified according to duration

The redundancy series commenced with the June 1973 issue of the *Statistical Bulletin*. Redundancy figures are presented in each issue of the Bulletin as:

- number of redundancies notified by employers during the twelve months ended December.

Central Statistics Office
STATISTICAL RELEASES
Dublin: Central Statistics Office

Statistical Releases issued by the Central Statistics Office update the information and statistics in the *Statistical Bulletin*. Listed below are the *Releases* issued for the labour force, unemployment and industrial disputes.

- Labour force preliminary estimate (annually)
- Live Register statement (monthly)
- Live Register flow analysis (monthly)
- Live Register area analysis (monthly)
- Live Register age – by duration analysis (biannually)
- Industrial disputes (quarterly)

Listed below are the *Releases* issued for employment.

Industrial employment (quarterly)
Coverage includes total persons engaged in industrial establishments with 3 or more persons engaged and persons engaged in non-industrial activities.

Industrial earnings and hours worked (quarterly)

Industrial employment, earnings and hours worked (quarterly)

Banking, insurance and building societies – employment and earnings (quarterly)

Public sector employment (quarterly)

Sectors covered are: the civil service, defence forces, Garda Síochána, Local Authorities, education (excluding private institutions), semi-State bodies

Public sector average earnings index (quarterly)

Average earnings and hours worked in building and construction (quarterly)

Index of Employment in Building and Construction (monthly)

Department of Finance
ECONOMIC REVIEW AND OUTLOOK
Dublin: Stationery Office (annually)

The appendix in the *Economic Review and Outlook* comprises statistical tables with comparative figures for approximately nine years. Tables relevant to the labour force, numbers at work and earnings are:

- labour force
- hourly earnings indices.

Department of Foreign Affairs
DEVELOPMENTS IN THE EUROPEAN UNION
Dublin: Stationery Office (biannually)

In accordance with Section 5 of the 1972 European Communities Act, the Government is required to submit twice yearly to each House of the Oireachtas a report on developments in the European Communities. Topics relevant to employment include:

- protection of workers
- payments from the European Social Fund for vocational training
- employment schemes
- youth employment
- Operational Programme for Human Resource Development
- employment incentive schemes.

Other Publications: Irish

FÁS - Training and Employment Authority
ANNUAL REPORT AND FINANCIAL STATEMENTS
Dublin: FÁS (annually)

The principal functions of FÁS are set out in the Labour Services Act, 1987. In the *Annual Report* the Chairman's Statement gives a review of the performance and activities of FÁS.

The Director General's Statement comments on:

- the Irish economy, growth in employment and the types of work the Irish labour force is engaged in

- the wide range of vocational training services provided by FÁS to communities and unemployed persons
- success of the Community Employment Programmes in providing work and training opportunities for disadvantaged persons in the Irish labour market
- FÁS services to jobseekers
- FÁS services to businesses
- training schemes and placement schemes offered by FÁS
- FÁS Local Enterprise Programme
- work of the Industrial Training Committees
- throughput for FÁS programmes by region statistics.

Forfás
EMPLOYMENT SURVEY
Dublin: Forfás (annually)

Forfás is the policy advisory and co-ordination board for industrial development and science and technology in Ireland. The *Employment Survey* comprises text supported by charts and tables summarised below.

- net change in employment and resulting total employment
- survey results of the previous year
- highlights of the past ten years
- international trends in manufacturing employment
- overall trends, Irish-owned and foreign-owned components
- overall trends, manufacturing and internationally traded service components
- manufacturing employment: overall trends
- internationally traded services employment: overall trends, Irish-owned and foreign-owned components
- job gains, job losses and net change trends
- Irish-owned employment: job gains, job losses and net change trends
- foreign-owned employment: job gains, job losses and net change trends
- temporary, part-time and short-term contract employment trends
- permanent full-time employment: regional trends
- permanent full-time employment: sectoral trends
- temporary, part-time and short-term contract employment: regional trends
- temporary, part-time and short-term contract employment: sectoral trends
- international employment trends

Publications: International Organisations

European Communities, Commission
EMPLOYMENT IN EUROPE
Luxembourg: Office for Official Publications of the European Communities (annually)
Employment in Europe 1997 is the ninth of the series. It covers a wide range of issues, examples of which are listed below.

- employment and unemployment developments
- prospects for employment
- job creation schemes and measures
- labour force trends

- labour market policies
- subsidised employment in EU Member States
- promotion of equal opportunities for women

Tables of employment indicators for EU Member States give figures for the following (eight year period).

- total population
- population of working age (15–64)
- total employment
- annual change in employment (%)
- annual change in GDP/employed (%)
- employment rate (% population 15–64)
- self-employment (% employed)
- employed on fixed-term contracts (% employees)
- share of employment in agriculture (%)
- share of employment in industry (%)
- share of employment in services (%)
- activity rate (% population 15–64)
- total unemployed
- unemployment rate (% labour force)
- youth unemployed (% labour force 15–24)
- long-term unemployment (% unemployed)
- 15–19-year-olds in education/training (%)
- 20–24-year-olds in education/training (%)

European Communities, Eurostat (Statistical Office of the EC)
EARNINGS – INDUSTRY AND SERVICES
Luxembourg: Office for Official Publications of the European Communities (annually)

Earnings – Industry and Services gives harmonised statistics on the earnings of manual and non-manual workers in industry and in the services sector. Listed below are selected tables.

Statistics of earnings of manual workers in industry
- average gross hourly earnings of manual workers, by major industrial group
- trends of average gross hourly earnings of manual workers, by industrial group
- average gross hourly earnings of manual workers by industrial group in respect of each Member State of the EU

Statistics of earnings of non-manual workers in industry
- average gross monthly earnings of non-manual workers in industry
- trends of average gross monthly earnings
- average gross monthly earnings of non-manual workers by industrial group in respect of each Member State of the EU

European Communities, Eurostat (Statistical Office of the EC)
EMPLOYMENT AND UNEMPLOYMENT – aggregates
Luxembourg: Office for Official Publications of the European Communities (annually)

This bulletin sets out to provide a comprehensive view of the labour market in the European Union.

Figures are given for all the EU Member States, United States and Japan, for the following.

Selected indicators
- total number of persons in employment over the age of 15 (males and females)
- numbers unemployed (males and females)
- proportion of women employed in each sector of economic activity (%)
- proportion of employees in each sector of economic activity (%)
- proportion of sectors of economic activity in total employment (%)

Population and active population
- total population by sex
- total active population by sex

Employment
- total employment by sex
- employment by sex and sector of economic activity
- employers, self-employed and family workers by sex and sector of economic activity

Unemployment
- unemployment rates by sex and age category – annual averages (%)
- unemployment by sex and age category – annual averages
- unemployment of one or more years' duration as a proportion of total unemployment, by sex and age category at time of survey (%)
- persons registered at employment offices, by sex and age category – annual averages

European Communities, Eurostat (Statistical Office of the EC)
LABOUR COSTS (two volumes)
Luxembourg: Office for Official Publications of the European Communities (every four years + updating bulletins)

The *Labour Cost Survey 1988* was published in 1992. Explanatory notes and conversion tables accompany the tables.

Industries and services are classified according to the general industrial classification of economic activities (NACE)

Volume 1: Principal results: industry and services

The tables in this volume have data on labour costs and the structure of labour costs in industry and services. Service industries include commerce, banking and insurance. Examples are:

- monthly labour costs: manual and non-manual workers (in national currency and in ECUs)
- hourly labour costs: manual and non-manual workers (in national currency and in ECUs)
- monthly earnings: manual and non-manual workers (in national currency and in ECUs)
- monthly earnings: manual and non-manual workers (in purchasing power standards, PPS)
- numbers of manual and non-manual workers: full-time and part-time
- number of women workers: full-time and part-time
- number of women as a percentage of the total workforce

- structure of labour costs in establishments of 10 or more employees and in establishments of 50 or more employees

Volume 2: Results by size classes and by regions

The tables in this volume present the principal results of labour costs by size of establishment and by region. The information is similar to that given in Volume 1.

European Communities, Eurostat (Statistical Office of the EC)
LABOUR COSTS – Principal Results
Luxembourg: Office for Official Publications of the European Communities (every four years + updating bulletins)

The *Labour Costs – Principal Results 1992* survey was published in 1997. Certain revisions mean that the 1992 survey is not totally comparable with the preceding surveys. It contains three principal sections, summarised below.

General tables: industry and services
- monthly labour costs in national currency
- monthly labour costs in ECUs
- hourly labour costs in national currency
- hourly labour costs in ECUs
- monthly direct remunerations in national currency
- hourly direct remunerations in national currency
- average number of hours worked during the year
- average number of hours worked by part-time employees during the year

Structure of costs: industry
- structure of labour costs as per cent of total costs

Structure of costs: services
- structure of labour costs as per cent of total costs

European Communities, Eurostat (Statistical Office of the EC)
LABOUR COSTS – Updating
Luxembourg: Office for Official Publications of the European Communities (annually)

In the *Labour Costs – Updating Bulletin 1992–1995*, the Statistical Office of the European Communities presents the 1993, 1994 and 1995 updating of the main results of the 1992 survey on labour costs. The estimates refer to the average cost of all manual and non-manual workers in local units or enterprises employing at least ten persons.

European Communities, Eurostat (Statistical Office of the EC)
LABOUR FORCE SURVEY – Results
Luxembourg: Office for Official Publications of the European Communities (annually)

The 1995 *Labour Force Survey* is the fourth survey in a new series. Explanatory notes precede the graphs and tables. Examples are listed below.

Population and activity
- activity by sex and age groups
- population aged 25–59 years with third-level education
- activity of young persons aged 15 to 24 years
- principal characteristics of activity of the population (numbers and %)
- activity rates by age groups (%)
- activity rates by marital status and broad age groups (%)
- activity rates by nationality and broad age groups (%)
- employment/population ratios by age groups (%)
- unemployment rates by age groups (%)
- total population by age groups
- labour force by age groups
- labour force by age groups (%)
- persons in employment by age groups
- persons in employment by age groups (%)
- employment status by educational attainment level of persons aged 25 to 59 years
- employment status by educational attainment level of persons aged 25 to 29 years (%)

Employment
- employment/population rate (1990 and 1995) – EUR15 – males
- employment/population rate (1990 and 1995) – EUR15 – females
- persons in employment by sector of economic activity
- share of industrial sector in total employment
- share of services sector in total employment
- persons in employment by professional status
- persons in employment by professional status and sector of activity (%)
- persons in employment by sector of activity and professional status
- persons in employment by economic activity
- persons in employment by occupation
- persons working full-time/part-time by broad age groups
- persons working full-time/part-time by broad age groups (%)
- persons in employment by professional status and full-time/part-time breakdown
- persons in employment by sector of activity and full-timer part-time breakdown (%)
- persons working shift work
- persons working shift work (%)
- reasons for total absence from work during the reference week
- persons in employment with more than one job by sector of activity of the second job (%)
- average hours usually worked per week (males)
- average hours usually worked per week (females)
- shift work, night work, Saturday work, Sunday work
- persons in employment – comparison of average usual and average actual number of hours worked by sector of activity
- employees working full-time – average hours usually worked per week by occupation
- employees working part-time – average hours usually worked per week by economic activity
- persons in full-time employment – groups of hours actually worked during the reference week (%)
- employees in industry and services working part-time – groups of hours usually worked per week (%)

Unemployment and search for work
- employment rate and percentage of long-term unemployed

- principal characteristics of the unemployed
- principal characteristics of the young unemployed
- duration of unemployment for the main groups of unemployed
- duration of unemployment by broad age groups
- unemployed seeking employment by broad age group and type of employment sought

Households
- composition of private households
- activity rates and unemployment rates by household type
- number of private households by age of youngest person in the household (%)

International Labour Organisation (ILO)
BULLETIN OF LABOUR STATISTICS
Geneva: International Labour Office (annually)
The *Bulletin of Labour Statistics* updates the statistics in the *Yearbook of Labour Statistics*. In each bulletin, the tables are preceded by an article in the field of labour economics. Figures are given for the following.

Employment
- general level of employment
- paid employment in non-agricultural activities
- paid employment in manufacturing industries

Unemployment
- general level of unemployment

Hours of work
- hours of work per week in non-agricultural activities
- hours of work per week in manufacturing

Wages
- wages in non-agricultural activities
- wages in manufacturing

Consumer prices

International Labour Organisation (ILO)
SUPPLEMENT TO THE BULLETIN OF LABOUR STATISTICS
Geneva: International Labour Office (quarterly)

This supplement comprises tables and updates the data in the *Bulletin of Labour Statistics*. The data in the supplement are incorporated in each new issue of the bulletin.

International Labour Organisation (ILO)
YEARBOOK OF LABOUR STATISTICS
Geneva: International Labour Office (annually)

The *Yearbook of Labour Statistics* is international in scope and includes approximately 190 countries arranged in alphabetical order within each continent. It is updated by the *Bulletin of Labour*

Statistics. Explanatory notes precede the statistical tables, which contain figures for the following.

Employment
- economically active population by age group and by level of education
- total employment by economic activity, by occupation, by status in employment
- paid employment by economic activity and in manufacturing industry

Unemployment
- unemployment by age group, by level of education, by economic activity, by occupation

Hours of work
- by economic activity and in manufacturing industry

Wages
- by economic activity and in manufacturing industry

Labour cost
- cost of labour in manufacturing industry

Consumer prices
- general indices and indices for food, fuel and light, clothing and rent

Occupational injuries

Strikes and lockouts
- strikes and lockouts by economic activity and by days not worked

Organisation for Economic Co-operation and Development (OECD)
EMPLOYMENT OUTLOOK
Paris: OECD (annually)

This provides an annual assessment of labour market developments and prospects in OECD member countries. Each issue contains an overall analysis of the latest labour market trends and short-term forecasts and examines key labour market developments.

The text is supported by tables, graphs and charts. Examples of topics covered are:

- labour market developments
- recent economic trends
- wages, unit labour costs and inflation
- developments in employment by occupation
- unemployment rates by occupation
- labour force, employment and unemployment trends
- public expenditure in labour market programmes
- labour force projections
- labour market policies
- monthly flows into and out of unemployment
- youth unemployment.

The statistical annexe in each issue contains detailed tables. A bibliography is also included.

Organisation for Economic Co-operation and Development (OECD)
LABOUR FORCE STATISTICS YEARBOOK
Paris: OECD (annually + quarterly supplements)

The *Labour Force Statistics Yearbook* comprises three parts preceded by a section on definitions and sources of data.

Part 1 – General tables and graphs (12-year period)
Contain figures for:

- total population for each OECD country, OECD – Europe, OECD – total
- total labour force
- total labour force as a percentage of total population
- total employment
- civilian labour force
- numbers employed in the armed forces
- unemployment – total
- employment by sector
- unemployment as percentage of total labour force

Part 2 – Country tables (12-year period)
- population
- total labour force
- civilian employment
- wage earners and salaried employees by activities

Part 3
- participation rates and unemployment rates by age and sex

Organisation for Economic Co-operation and Development (OECD)
QUARTERLY LABOUR FORCE STATISTICS
Paris: OECD (quarterly)

This provides short-term data. Tables for selected OECD countries are supported by graphs and charts, and give figures for:

- total labour force (males and females)
- employment by sector (agriculture, industry and services)
- unemployment (males and females)
- youth unemployment.

United Nations. Department for Economic and Social Information and Policy Analysis
STATISTICAL YEARBOOK
New York: United Nations (annually)

The *Statistical Yearbook* is international in scope. Countries are listed in alphabetical order. Figures for the labour force are contained in the following tables:

- employment by industry (total employment; numbers employed in agriculture, forestry and fishing; mining and quarrying; manufacturing industries; electricity, gas, water;

construction; hotels and catering; transport and communications; financial services sector; community, social and personal services)
- unemployment
- wages: earnings in manufacturing.

National Accounts

Central Statistics Office
ECONOMIC SERIES
Dublin: Stationery Office (monthly)

The *Economic Series* bulletin provides up-to-date information and five years' retrospection for a selection of 151 principal short-term economic series. Longer retrospection is given in each December issue.

Charts and graphs accompany the tables. The numbers pertaining to national accounts are as follows:

8.06	Total revenue receipts
8.07	Total Exchequer expenditure
8.08	Current Budget deficit
8.09	Exchequer Borrowing Requirement

Central Statistics Office
INPUT–OUTPUT TABLES
Dublin: Stationery Office (periodically)

The *Input–Output Tables* for 1990 were published in 1997. These tables provide a statistical description of the inputs and outputs of the different branches of the economy and their inter-relationships. Previously published tables referred to the years 1964, 1969, 1975 and 1985. Essential features of the input–output tables precede the tables themselves.

Tables – 1990 input–output 41-branch analysis
Table 1 – At basic prices, with imports shown separately
Table 2 – Direct input coefficients
Table 3 – Inverse of domestic flows with multipliers for other inputs
Table 4 – Detailed distribution of merchandise imports
Table 5 – Transactions at producers' prices for domestic and import flows combined

Central Statistics Office
NATIONAL INCOME AND EXPENDITURE
Dublin: Stationery Office (annually)

National Income and Expenditure 1996, published in 1997, includes preliminary estimates of the national accounts for the year 1996 together with more detailed data for the years 1990 to 1995. The tables relate to national income and expenditure, capital formation and savings together with details of transactions of the Government sector classified in accordance with national accounting definitions.

It comprises text, detailed tables and diagrams. The tables are summarised below.

- net national product at factor cost, 1990–1996

- net domestic product at factor cost by sector of origin and Gross National Product at current market prices, 1990–1996
- expenditure on Gross National Product at current market prices, 1990–1996
- gross national disposable income and its use, 1990–1996
- personal income and personal expenditure, 1990–1995
- net current income and expenditure of public authorities, 1990–1996
- savings and capital formation, 1990–1996
- consumption of personal income at current market prices, 1990–1996
- gross domestic fixed capital formation by sector of use at current market prices, 1990–1996
- receipts and expenditure of central government, 1990–1995
- receipts and expenditure of local authorities, 1990–1995
- receipts and expenditure of public authorities, 1990–1995
- details of subsidies and capital grants to enterprises, 1990–1995
- details of taxation, 1990–1995
- expenditure of central government classified by purpose of expenditure and economic category, 1990–1995
- expenditure of local authorities classified by purpose of expenditure and economic category, 1990–1995
- social protection accounts, 1990–1995
- balance of international payments: current account
- balance of international payments: capital and financial account and net residual

Central Statistics Office
STATISTICAL ABSTRACT
Dublin: Stationery Office (annually)

Each issue of the *Statistical Abstract* contains a section on national accounts. The tables are supported by an explanatory text. Examples from the 1996 *Statistical Abstract* are as follows:

- Net National Product at factor cost, 1990–1995
- Net National Product at factor cost by sectors of origin, 1990–1995
- Gross National Product at current and constant (1990) market prices, 1990–1995
- consumption of personal income at current market prices, 1990–1995
- consumption of personal income at constant (1990) market prices, 1990–1995
- details of gross domestic fixed capital formation, 1990–1995

Central Statistics Office
STATISTICAL RELEASES
Dublin: Central Statistics Office

Statistical Releases issued by the Central Statistics Office update the information and statistics in the *Statistical Bulletin*. The release issued for national income and expenditure is:

- National income and expenditure – first results (annually).

Department of Finance
ECONOMIC REVIEW AND OUTLOOK
Dublin: Stationery Office (annually)

The appendix in the *Economic Review and Outlook* comprises statistical tables with comparative figures for approximately nine years. Tables relevant to finance are:

- Gross National Product and Gross Domestic Product at current market prices and percentage change in GNP and GDP at constant (1990) prices
- expenditure on GNP at current market prices
- expenditure on GNP at constant (1990) market prices
- GDP at factor cost by sector of origin and GNP at current market prices
- GDP at factor cost by sector of origin and GNP at constant (1990) market prices
- Net Domestic Product at factor cost by sector of origin and GNP at current market prices
- national income
- national disposable income, savings and capital formation
- general Government deficit.

Publications: International Organisations

European Communities, Eurostat (Statistical Office of the EC)
GENERAL GOVERNMENT ACCOUNTS AND STATISTICS
Luxembourg: Office for Official Publications of the European Communities (annually)

General Government Accounts and Statistical 1970–1993 was published in 1995 and contains the results of the national accounts of Member States, drawn up in accordance with the European system of Integrated Accounts (ESA). The statistics show all transactions of general government broken down by subsector (central government, local government, social security funds) together with an analysis of public income and expenditure. The volume also presents detailed information on the receipts from various national taxes.

The statistical tables are supported by graphs and charts. Examples are:

- net lending of General Government in % of GDP 1993
- receipts of General Government in % of GDP 1982–1993
- current and capital expenditure of General Government in % of GDP 1982–1993
- current and capital expenditure of General Government by subsector
- current and capital expenditure of General Government by category.

European Communities, Eurostat (Statistical Office of the EC)
NATIONAL ACCOUNTS: ESA: aggregates
Luxembourg: Office for Official Publications of the European Communities (annually)

National Accounts: ESA: aggregates 1970–1994 was published in 1996 and brings together the economic and financial accounts of the institutional sectors for the 15 Member States of the EU, United States of America and Japan. The accounts have been compiled in accordance with the European System of Integrated Economic Accounts (ESA). Selected tables are listed below.

- main aggregates (in ECUs)
- origin and use of goods and services (in ECUs)
- main aggregates (in PPS)
- origin and use of goods and services (in PPS)
- GDP at market prices
- GDP at market prices, in current and constant prices
- final national consumption

- private national consumption
- collective consumption of general Government
- gross fixed capital formation
- exports
- imports
- balance of exports and imports
- compensation of wage and salary earners
- consumption of fixed capital
- net national disposable income
- net national saving
- ECU exchange rates and purchasing power parities
- private and national consumption
- collective consumption of general Government
- gross fixed capital formation
- volume and price indices

European Communities, Eurostat (Statistical Office of the EC)
NATIONAL ACCOUNTS: ESA: detailed tables by branch
Luxembourg: Office for Official Publications of the European Communities (annually)

National Accounts: ESA: detailed tables by branch 1970–1994 was published in 1996. It contains the seven main aggregates of the national accounts of the 15 Member States of the EU as listed:

- gross value added at market prices (by ownership branch)
- total employment (by ownership branch)
- paid employment [wage and salary earners] (by ownership branch)
- compensation of employees (by ownership branch)
- gross fixed capital formation (by investment product)
- gross fixed capital formation (by ownership branch)
- final consumption of households (by purpose).

It also includes exchange rates of the ECU 1970–1994.

European Communities, Eurostat (Statistical Office of the EC)
NATIONAL ACCOUNTS: ESA: detailed tables by sector – non-financial transactions
Luxembourg: Office for Official Publications of the European Communities (annually)

The *National Accounts: ESA: detailed tables by sector 1983–1994* yearbook was published in 1996. Explanatory notes and definitions precede the tables which are based on the European system of Integrated Economic Accounts (ESA). The tables contain detailed data for the Member States of the EU on flows of income between sectors (household, government, enterprises, etc.). They have been grouped into two main sections as listed below.

Comparative tables
Main aggregates
- Gross Domestic Product (GDP) in the EU
- Gross Domestic Product (GDP) in the EU and its generation
- Gross Domestic Product (GDP) and its uses
- Gross Domestic Product (GDP) and its distribution
- Gross Domestic Product (GDP) and its distribution by sector

- compensation of employees by sector
- gross national disposable income and its uses
- net lending of the sectors

Households and non-profit institutions
- generation of disposable income
- uses of the disposable income
- use of gross saving
- unrequited current transfers received in % of the current receipts
- gross saving in % of the disposable income
- net lending (+) or net borrowing (–) in % of the disposable income

Enterprises
- generation of the disposable income
- net lending in % of gross saving
- gross disposable income in % of current receipts
- gross capital accumulation in % of current receipts

General Government
- generation of disposable income
- uses of disposable income
- actual interest in % of current receipts
- final national consumption in % of current receipts
- gross capital accumulation in % of GDP
- net lending in % of GDP

Country tables – EU Member States
Simplified accounts
National economy (goods and services account, production account, generation of income account, distribution of income account, use of income account, capital account)

Overview of sector accounts

Sector accounts
Households and private non-profit institutions, non-financial enterprises

Data for Ireland are contained in Part 1 of the 1993–1994 yearbook and in Parts 1 and 2 of the 1981–1992 yearbook.

European Communities, Eurostat (Statistical Office of the EC)
QUARTERLY NATIONAL ACCOUNTS – ESA
Luxembourg: Office for Official Publications of the European Communities (quarterly)

Each issue of this bulletin contains a brief commentary on the economic situation in the EU Member States and economic developments in the EU's main trading partners, i.e. the United States, Japan, Canada and Australia.

Part 2 of the bulletin comprises tables and charts for the EU Member States for:

- GDP and its components – current prices
- GDP and its components – 1990 prices.

Organisation for Economic Co-operation and Development (OECD)
NATIONAL ACCOUNTS OF OECD COUNTRIES (2 volumes)
Paris: OECD (annually)

National Accounts of OECD Countries mainly comprises the tables summarised below.

Volume 1: Main aggregates (30-year period)
- expenditure on the GDP
- cost components of the GDP
- capital transactions of the nation (finance of gross capital formation; gross capital formation)
- relations among national accounting aggregates

Growth triangles
- per capita GDP (volume)
- per capita private consumption (volume)
- GDP (volume and implicit price deflator)
- private final consumption expenditure
- Government final consumption expenditure
- gross fixed capital formation
- national disposable income (value)
- compensation of employees (value)

Comparative tables based on exchange rates
- Gross Domestic Product
- Gross Domestic Product per head
- private final consumption expenditure
- Government final consumption expenditure
- gross fixed capital formation
- exports/imports of goods and services

Volume 2: Detailed tables for each OECD member country (13-year period)
- main aggregates
- private final consumption expenditure by type and purpose
- gross fixed capital formation by kind of activity of owner
- gross capital formation by type of good and owner
- accounts for General Government (Central Government and Local Government)
- accounts for social security funds
- external transactions, current and capital accumulation accounts
- Gross Domestic Product by kind of activity
- cost components of value added by kind of activity
- profit shares and rates of return on capital

Organisation for Economic Co-operation and Development (OECD)
QUARTERLY NATIONAL ACCOUNTS
Paris: OECD (quarterly)

Quarterly National Accounts provides information on the main national accounts aggregates for all OECD member countries which prepare national accounts on a quarterly basis and on a selected number of aggregates for five groups of member countries. It is divided into three parts.

Part 1
- OECD – total
- NAFTA – Canada, Mexico and United States
- OECD – Europe
- Major Seven

Part 2 – Tables by country
The data for each country are given in tables:
- Gross Domestic Product by type of expenditure
- GDP by cost structure
- financing for gross capital formation
- composition of gross capital formation
- private consumption expenditure by type of expenditure
- private consumption expenditure by object.

Part 3 – Comparative tables

United Nations. Department for Economic and Social Information and Policy Analysis
NATIONAL ACCOUNTS STATISTICS: main aggregates and detailed tables
New York: United Nations (annually)

This yearbook contains detailed national accounts estimates for 184 countries and areas. Data are compiled in accordance with the United Nations System of National Accounts (SNA). Listed below are examples from each part of the yearbook.

Part 1: Summary information
- expenditures on the Gross Domestic Product (current prices)
- expenditures on the Gross Domestic Product (constant prices)
- cost components of the Gross Domestic Product
- general Government current receipts and expenditures
- current income and outlay of corporate and quasi-corporate enterprises
- current income and outlay of households and non-profit institutions
- Gross Domestic Product by kind of activity (current prices)
- Gross Domestic Product by kind of activity (constant prices)

Part 2: Final expenditures on Gross Domestic Product
- general Government final consumption expenditure by function (current prices)
- general Government final consumption expenditure by function (constant prices)
- private final consumption expenditure by type (current prices)
- private final consumption expenditure by type (constant prices)
- gross capital formation by type of good and owner (current prices)
- gross capital formation by type of good and owner (constant prices)
- gross fixed capital formation by kind of activity of owner (current prices)
- gross fixed capital formation by kind of activity of owner (constant prices)
- stocks of reproducible fixed assets by type of good and owner (current prices)
- stocks of reproducible fixed assets by type of good and owner (constant prices)
- exports and imports of goods and services, detail

Part 3: Institutional sector accounts
General government
- production account: total and subsectors

- income and outlay account
- capital accumulation account
- capital finance account

Corporate and quasi-corporate enterprises
- production account: total and sectors
- income and outlay account
- capital accumulation account
- balance sheet
- financial transactions of financial institutions

Households and private enterprises
- production account
- income and outlay account
- capital accumulation account
- capital finance account
- balance sheet

External transactions
- current account
- capital accumulation account

Production by kind of activity
- derivation of value added by kind of activity (current prices)
- derivation of value added by kind of activity (constant prices)
- cost components of value added

United Nations. Department for Economic and Social Information and Policy Analysis
STATISTICAL YEARBOOK
New York: United Nations (annually)

The *Statistical Yearbook* is international in scope. Countries are listed in alphabetical order. Figures for national accounts are contained in the following tables.

- Gross Domestic Product: total and per capita
- expenditure on Gross Domestic Product at current prices
- Gross Domestic Product by kind of economic activity at current prices
- relationships between the principal national accounting aggregates
- Government final consumption expenditure by function at current prices

Population

Central Statistics Office
CENSUS OF POPULATION 1991 (10 volumes)
Dublin: Central Statistics Office (every five years)

The *Census of Population 1991* is the most recent complete Census, as described below. The volumes containing information of most relevance to the Irish economy are described in greater detail.

Volume 1 – Population classified by area
This volume gives the population classified by sex in each province, county, county borough, town, district electoral division, urban district, rural district, Gaeltacht area, inhabited island, county electoral area and constituency in Ireland. Information is also provided on marriages, births, deaths, natural population increase and estimated net migration in each province for each intercensal period since 1926.

Examples of tables
- population of each province, county and county borough at each census since 1971 and percentage change in each intercensal period
- population of each province and county as constituted at each census since 1841
- population of towns by type of district, 1986 and 1991
- persons, males and females in towns by type of district, 1991
- alphabetical list of towns with their population in 1991

Volume 2 – Age and marital status
This volume classifies the population in each province, county, county borough, town, urban district and rural district according to sex, age group and marital status. The average annual rate of change in the numbers of males and females in each age group in each intercensal period since 1966 is also shown.

Volume 3 – Household composition and family units
This volume provides details of the numbers of persons in private and non-private households in each province, county and county borough, distinguishing between households in permanent housing units and those in temporary housing units. All private households and those in permanent housing units are classified by type, number of persons, age, sex and marital status of head of household.

Volume 4 – Principal economic status and industries
This volume classifies persons aged 15 years and over by principal economic status (i.e. employed, unemployed, students, etc.), sex, age group and marital status. Results for the principal economic status and sex classifications are published for each province, planning region, county and county borough. The persons at work in each province, planning region, county, county borough, urban and rural districts and large towns are classified by industrial group and sex.

Examples of tables
- rates of participation in the labour force for persons, males and females classified by age group and marital status
- persons, males and females at work classified by industrial .group with numbers in each group per 10,000 in all industries

- males and females at work in each industry, distinguishing the principal occupations within that industry
- population at work classified by industrial group and employment status showing also the numbers out of work in each industrial group

Volume 5 – Religion

Volume 6 – Occupations

This volume relating to the labour force provides details of the number of males and females in each province, county, county borough, urban and rural district and large town classified by occupational group. Males and females in each occupational group in each province, county and county borough are also classified by age group. Males and females out of work, having lost or given up a previous job, are classified by age group and occupational group.

Examples of tables

- persons, males and females in each occupational group per 10,000 in the labour force
- persons, males and females classified by occupation
- males and females classified by occupation and employment status including unemployed persons classified by former occupation
- population out of work, having lost or given up previous job, classified by age group and former occupational group

Volume 7 – An Ghaeilge/Irish language

Volume 8 – Usual residence and migration, birthplaces

Volume 9 – Education

Volume 10 – Housing

This volume contains tables relating to housing and social amenities and is in two parts. Part 1 refers to private households/dwellings in permanent housing units and Part 2 covers permanent housing units.

Examples of tables (Part 1)

- persons in private and non-private households in each province, county and county borough
- private households in permanent housing units in each province and county classified by the number of rooms occupied – 1946 to 1991
- persons in private households in permanent housing units, classified by number of persons per room
- private dwellings classified by nature of occupancy, period in which built, type of building in which situated and distinguishing number of persons in these dwellings
- rented private dwellings in each planning section, classified by weekly rent and number of rooms occupied
- private dwellings in each planning region, classified by nature of occupancy, principal method of heating and principal type of fuel used
- farm dwellings in each province, county and county borough, period in which built, water supply, sanitary facilities, etc.

Examples of tables (Part 2)

- private housing units, private households, persons and rooms by type of building
- permanent private housing units, classified by water supply, sanitary facilities, type of building

in which situated and distinguishing number of persons in these housing units
- permanent private housing units classified by nature of occupancy
- rented permanent private housing units classified by weekly rent
- permanent private housing units classified by period in which built
- permanent private housing units classified by sanitary facilities and showing number having indoor toilet

Central Statistics Office
CENSUS OF POPULATION OF IRELAND 1996
Dublin: Stationery Office

Preliminary report
The preliminary report of the Census 1996 has information on:
- coverage of the Census
- total population and population of provinces
- population of counties and county boroughs
- ratio of females to males
- net migration
- components of population changes, 1926–1996.

Examples of tables
- population of each province and county, 1926–1996
- population of each urban and rural district, 1991–1996
- population of each county, county borough, urban district, rural district, district electoral division and ward, 1991–1996
- components of population change for each Regional Authority, 1991–1996
- components of population change for each province, county and county borough, 1991–1996

Volume 1 – Population classified by area
Examples of tables
- population of each province, county and county borough and actual and percentage change, 1991–1996
- population of towns ordered by county and size, 1991 and 1996
- persons, males and females in the aggregate town and aggregate rural areas of each province, county and county borough and percentage of population in aggregate town area, 1996
- population of inhabited islands off the coast, 1991 and 1996
- alphabetical list of towns with their population, 1991 and 1996

Central Statistics Office
CENSUS 1996: PRINCIPAL DEMOGRAPHIC RESULTS
Dublin: Stationery Office

Census 1996: Principal Demographic Results, published in 1997, has information on:

- coverage of the Census
- small area population statistics (SAPS)
- geographic distribution of the population
- age and sex composition

- marital status
- living arrangements
- migration.

Examples of tables
- persons, males and females in the State at each census since 1841
- persons, males and females classified by age group at each census since 1926
- population of each province, county and county borough, 1991 and 1996
- persons classified by age group, sex and marital status in towns and rural areas
- population in each province, county and county borough classified by age group – persons, males and females
- number of private households classified by composition and size
- persons, males and females classified by usual residence
- family units in private households classified by type of family unit and number of children

This report includes the 1996 Census questionnaire.

Central Statistics Office
CENSUS 1996 – PRINCIPAL SOCIO-ECONOMIC RESULTS
Dublin: Stationery Office

A Census of Population was taken on 28 April 1996. The *Principal Socio-economic Results* report gives the final census results for the State as a whole for travel patterns, the Irish language, education and labour force characteristics. Coverage of the Census, conduct of the Census and production of results precede the two principal sections of this report, summarised below.

Commentary (text plus tables)

Principal economic status
- population aged 15 years and over classified by principal economic status and sex, 1991 and 1996
- main labour market indicators, 1971–1996
- labour force participation rates for females aged 20 to 49, 1996

Employment
- sectoral employment shares 1926–1996
- persons at work classified by industrial group, 1996
- occupations with highest segregation
- employment status of persons at work classified by sex, 1991 and 1996
- part-time work

Unemployment
- unemployment rates by age group and sex, 1996
- distribution of unemployment blackspots by county, 1996
- long-term unemployment

Education
- percentage of persons aged 15 to 24 years receiving full-time education

Travel patterns
- means of travel to work, 1981–1996
- average distance travelled to work, school or college, 1981–1996

Central Statistics Office
CENSUS 96
Dublin: Stationery Office

Four volumes of the *Census 1996* were published in 1997.

Volume 1: Population classified by area
Volume 2: Ages and marital status
Volume 3: Household composition and family units
Volume 4: Usual residence and migration, birthplaces

Central Statistics Office
ECONOMIC SERIES
Dublin: Stationery Office (monthly)

The *Economic Series* bulletin provides up-to-date information and five years' retrospection for a selection of 151 principal short-term economic series. Longer retrospection is given in each December issue. Charts and graphs accompany the tables. The numbers pertaining to vital statistics are as follows.

10.01	Marriages – number
10.02	Births – number
10.03	Deaths – number
10.04	Marriage rates – per 1,000 population
10.05	Birth rates – per 1,000 population
10.06	Death rates – per 1,000 population
10.07	Births outside marriage – number
10.08	Births outside marriage as a percentage of total births

---

Central Statistics Office
REPORT ON VITAL STATISTICS
Dublin: Stationery Office (annually)

The *Report on Vital Statistics* comprises text and detailed tables on the following.

Marriages
- number and rate, age at marriage, mode of celebration, socio-economic group, area of residence

Births
- number and rate, age at maternity, multiple births

Deaths
- number and rate, comparisons between counties, causes of death

Population
- estimated population in each year, 1951 onwards
- estimated population by age
- population by sex of each county and county borough according to the Census of Population, 1991

Central Statistics Office
STATISTICAL ABSTRACT
Dublin: Stationery Office (annually)

Each issue of the *Statistical Abstract* contains a section on population and vital statistics. The tables are supported by an explanatory text. Examples from the 1996 *Statistical Abstract* are listed below.

Population
- population of each province at each Census from 1841 to 1996
- number of births and deaths registered in each intercensal period since 1881
- population of each province, county and county borough – Censuses of Population
- population classified by sex and age group – Censuses of Population
- males and females classified by age group and marital status 1991

Vital statistics
- marriages, births and deaths and rates per 1,000 of the population 1989–1995
- persons enumerated in each county or county borough classified by country of birth – Census of Population 1991
- persons, males and females at work classified by industrial group – Census of Population 1991
- males and females at work classified by industry – Census of Population 1991
- estimated population classified by age and principal economic status, 1990–1996

Central Statistics Office
STATISTICAL BULLETIN + Index
Dublin: Stationery Office (quarterly)

Population and migration statistics are published in the March and December issues of the *Statistical Bulletin*. The tables give figures for:

- population classified by sex and age group
- estimated out-migration and in-migration classified by country of destination/origin and sex
- estimated out-migration and in-migration classified by age group and sex.

Figures for vital statistics – marriages, births and deaths – are presented in each issue of the *Statistical Bulletin*. The tables give figures for:

- marriages registered in each quarter, with the corresponding annual marriage rates per 1,000 population
- births registered in each quarter, with the corresponding annual birth rates per 1,000 population
- deaths registered in each quarter, with the corresponding annual death rates per 1,000

population
- infant deaths registered in each quarter, with the corresponding annual infant mortality rates per 1,000 live births
- births outside marriage registered in each quarter.

Central Statistics Office
STATISTICAL RELEASES
Dublin: Central Statistics office

Statistical Releases issued by the Central Statistics Office update the information and statistics in the *Statistical Bulletin*. The *Release* issued for demography is:

Population and migration estimates (annually).

Department of Finance
ECONOMIC REVIEW AND OUTLOOK
Dublin: Stationery Office (annually)

The appendix in the *Economic Review and Outlook* comprises statistical tables with comparative figures for approximately nine years. The relevant table for population is encaptioned

'Population, natural increase and net migration'.

Publications: International Organisations

Council of Europe
RECENT DEMOGRAPHIC DEVELOPMENTS IN EUROPE
Strasbourg: Council of Europe Press (annually)

This report is divided into three parts, summarised below.

Introduction
- the demographic situation in Europe
- main demographic indicators for Europe

Synopsis
- population and population change
- marriage and divorce
- fertility
- mortality

Country reports (Council of Europe Member States)
Text, maps, charts and graphs accompany the following tables:

- population by age and sex group
- births, deaths, marriages, divorces and legal abortions
- age-specific fertility rates and total fertility rate
- live births by order
- international migration

- population of foreign citizenship
- population change, natural increase and net migration.

European Communities, Eurostat (Statistical Office of the EC)
DEMOGRAPHIC STATISTICS
Luxembourg: Office for Official Publications of the European Communities (annually + updating supplements)

This bulletin comprises tables based on returns provided by the national authorities in Member States. Explanatory notes accompanied by a commentary on population change and structure precede the tables. Examples of tables are:

- population change
- population structure (numbers of males, females, population by age group, by citizenship, etc.)
- fertility rate
- marriage and divorce
- mortality rates
- migration statistics
- population projections.

Country reports on the demographic situation are also given.

United Nations. Department for Economic and Social Information and Policy Analysis. Statistics Division
DEMOGRAPHIC YEARBOOK
New York: United Nations (annually)

The *Demographic Yearbook* is a comprehensive collection of international demographic statistics. It covers approximately 233 countries and each edition includes a 'special topic'. Explanatory notes precede the tables arranged under the headings summarised below.

World summary
- population, rate of increase, birth and death rates
- estimates of population and its percentage distribution by age and sex and sex ratio for all ages
- population by sex, rate of population increase
- vital statistics summary and expectation of life at birth

Population
- estimation of mid-year population (ten-year period)
- urban and total population by sex
- population by age, sex and urban/rural residence
- population of capital cities and cities of 100,000 and more inhabitants

Nativity
- live births classified according to age of mother and by urban/rural residence

Foetal mortality

Infant and maternal mortality
- infant mortality rates by age, sex and urban/rural residence
- maternal deaths and maternal mortality rates

General mortality

Nuptiality

Divorces

Prices: Agricultural

Central Statistics Office
ECONOMIC SERIES
Dublin: Stationery Office (monthly)

The *Economic Series* bulletin provides up-to-date information and five years' retrospection for a selection of 151 principal short-term economic series. Longer retrospection is given in each December issue.

Charts and graphs accompany the tables. The numbers in this series pertaining to agricultural price indices are:

1.05	Total outputs index
1.06	Total outputs index (seasonally adjusted)
1.07	Livestock index
1.08	Livestock products index
1.09	Total inputs index
1.10	Total inputs index (seasonally adjusted)
1.11	Feedingstuffs index
1.12	Fertiliser index

Central Statistics Office
STATISTICAL ABSTRACT
Dublin: Stationery Office (annually)

Each issue of the *Statistical Abstract* contains a section on agricultural prices. The tables are supported by an explanatory text. Examples from the 1996 *Statistical Abstract* are:

- agricultural output price index 1990–1995
- agricultural input price index 1990–1995
- average price of bullocks and heifers at auction marts 1991–1995
- young pigs and sheep – average price per head and per live kg at auction marts 1991–1995
- price per litre paid by creameries to producers for milk 1991–1995.

Central Statistics Office
STATISTICAL BULLETIN + Index
Dublin: Stationery Office (quarterly)

Agricultural price index numbers and agricultural prices are published in each issue of the *Statistical Bulletin*. The tables are listed in the following order.

Agricultural Price Index
- agricultural price index (excluding VAT)
- agricultural output price index (excluding VAT)
- seasonally adjusted agricultural output price index (excluding VAT)
- agricultural input price index (excluding VAT)

- seasonally adjusted agricultural input price index (excluding VAT)

Agricultural prices
- average price of bullocks with a liveweight of 200 kg and over at livestock auction marts
- average price of heifers with a live weight of 200 kg and over at livestock auction marts
- average price of sheep at livestock auction marts
- average price of young pigs at livestock marts
- price per litre paid by creameries and producers for milk
- monthly and annual average retail prices of fertilisers
- monthly and annual average retail prices of feedingstuffs
- average retail prices of agricultural seeds (September issue)
- average annual prices of cereals and sugar beet

Central Statistics Office
STATISTICAL RELEASES
Dublin: Central Statistics Office

Statistical Releases issued by the Central Statistics Office update the information and statistics in the *Statistical Bulletin*. The *Releases* issued for agricultural prices are:

Agricultural Output Price Index (monthly)
Agricultural Input Price Index (monthly)

Other Publications: Irish

Irish Farm Centre
IRISH FARMERS JOURNAL
Dublin: Irish Farm Centre (weekly)

A section on prices called 'Market' is published each week in the *Irish Farmers Journal*. It contains details of the following.

Mart prices
- for store bullocks, beef bullocks, light bullocks, average all-cattle price

Mart reports
- prices for sheep, lambs and cattle at the major markets such as Athenry, Naas, Kilkenny, Dungarvan, Maynooth, Mullingar, Blessington, Middleton, with an analytical summary of the cattle trade at these markets
- factory cattle prices
- pig prices
- export factory disposals
- factory prices for cattle, sheep, lambs, etc.
- Department of Agriculture official prices for week ending ....

Publications: International Organisations

European Communities, Commission
AGRICULTURAL MARKETS – PRICES
Luxembourg: Office for Official Publications of the European Communities (monthly)

This bulletin comprises tables which contain price indices in respect of all the EU Member States for beef and veal; cereals; eggs and poultry; milk and milk products; mutton and lamb; olive oil; pigs and pigmeat; and rice.

European Communities, Eurostat (Statistical Office of the EC)
AGRICULTURAL PRICES – price indices and absolute prices
Luxembourg: Office for Official Publications of the European Communities (annually)

Agricultural Prices – price indices and absolute prices 1987–1996, published in 1997, contains annual data on agricultural price statistics and covers the previous ten years. Conversion rates and the rates of value-added tax in agriculture (1968–1995) precede the tables summarised below.

Agricultural prices
- selling prices of crop products (cereals and rice, potatoes, sugar beet, oilseeds)

Country tables
- selling prices of crop products (cereals and rice, root crops, fresh fruit, fresh vegetables, flowers)

United Nations. Economic Commission for Europe (ECE)
PRICES OF AGRICULTURAL PRODUCTS AND SELECTED INPUTS IN EUROPE AND NORTH AMERICA
Geneva: United Nations (annually)

This annual review is prepared by the Food and Agriculture Organization and Economic Commission for Europe (FAO/ECE). The overview of general changes in agricultural output and input prices in the ECE region is followed by statistical tables. Listed below are examples.

General changes in agricultural prices received by farmers
- indices of average prices received by farmers
- consumer price changes at December and June for 12-month periods

Prices of individual agricultural products
- ratios of pig prices to prices paid by farmers for feed for pigs
- ratios of prices of chickens for meat production to prices paid by farmers for feed
- ratios of egg prices to prices paid by farmers for feed for hens
- ratios of whole milk prices to prices paid by farmers for feed for dairy cows

Prices of selected inputs
- indices of average prices paid by farmers in a given year
- fixed-based price indices per unit of plant nutrient paid by farmers for fertilisers
- fixed-based indices of agricultural wage rates or labour costs
- average prices received by farmers for barley, oats, maize, potatoes, sugar beet, etc.
- average prices received by farmers for cattle for slaughter

Prices: Non-agricultural

Official Publications

Central Statistics Office
ECONOMIC SERIES
Dublin: Stationery Office (monthly)

The *Economic Series* bulletin provides up-to-date information and five years' retrospection for a selection of 151 principal short-term economic series. Longer retrospection is given in each December issue.

Charts and graphs accompany the tables. The numbers in this series pertaining to non-agricultural price indices are:

1.01	General wholesale price indices (excluding VAT)
1.02	Output price index (excluding VAT) for manufacturing industry
1.03	Building and construction materials index
1.04	Wholesale price index for petroleum products purchased by manufacturing industry
1.13	Consumer price index – all items
1.14	Consumer price index – food items
1.15	Consumer price index – energy products

Central Statistics Office
STATISTICAL ABSTRACT
Dublin: Stationery Office (annually)

Each issue of the *Statistical Abstract* contains a section on prices. The tables are supported by an explanatory text. Examples from the 1996 *Statistical Abstract* are listed below.

Consumer prices
- Consumer Price Index 1982–1995

Wholesale prices
- monthly output price indices (excluding VAT) for manufacturing industry 1991–1995
- industrial producer price indices 1992–1995
- wholesale price indices (excluding VAT) 1992–1995

Imports and exports
- import and export price (unit value) index numbers and terms of trade 1990–1995

Stocks and shares
- monthly price index numbers of ordinary stocks and shares (ISEQ) 1990–1995

Central Statistics Office
STATISTICAL BULLETIN + Index
Dublin: Stationery Office (quarterly)

Price index numbers, i.e. the consumer price index and wholesale price index numbers, are published in each issue of the *Statistical Bulletin* and the tables are listed in the following order.

Consumer Price Index
- consumer price Index (all items) base: 1989 = 100
- consumer price index (all items) base: 1968 = 100
- consumer price index (all items) base: 1914 = 100
- constant tax price index
- commodity group and all items – consumer price index numbers
- comparable national average retail prices

The EU *Interim Index of Consumer Prices* is published twice yearly in the June and December issues of *Statistical Bulletin*.

Wholesale Price Index
- wholesale price indices (excluding VAT)
- industrial production price indices (excluding VAT)
- wholesale price indices (excluding VAT) for building and construction materials
- capital goods price indices
- wholesale price indices (excluding VAT) for energy products

---

Central Statistics Office
STATISTICAL RELEASES
Dublin: Central Statistics Office

Statistical Releases issued by the Central Statistics Office update the information and statistics in the *Statistical Bulletin*. Listed below are the Releases issued for consumer prices and wholesale prices.

Consumer Price Index (quarterly)
Table 1: Consumer price index (all items)
Table 2: Consumer price commodity group indices

Wholesale Price Index (monthly)
Table 1: Wholesale price indices (excluding VAT)
Table 2: Industrial producer price indices (excluding VAT)
Table 3: Wholesale price indices (excluding VAT) for building and construction materials
Table 4: Capital goods price indices (excluding VAT)
Table 5: Wholesale price indices (excluding VAT) for energy products

---

Publications: International Organisations

European Communities, Eurostat (Statistical Office of the EC)
CONSUMER PRICE INDEX
Luxembourg: Office for Official Publications of the European Communities (monthly)

This bulletin comprises tables which give price indices for:

- durable goods
- rate of increase over one month
- rate of increase over 12 months

- annual average.

Price indices are given for the EU Member States, Switzerland, Iceland, Norway, Canada and the United States of America. The index for Ireland is quarterly.

Each issue for this bulletin contains a chart showing the annual inflation rate for each country.

European Communities, Eurostat (Statistical Office of the EC)
ELECTRICITY PRICES
Luxembourg: Office for Official Publications of the European Communities (annually)

Electricity Prices 1990–1996, published in 1997, comprises statistical tables. This report gives, for the three price levels concerned, prices in national currencies, ECUs and purchasing power standard (annual value as estimates for 1996). Coverage includes:

- market prices in national currencies
- electricity price indices for industry
- conversion factors and price indices
- comparative figures for selected cities and EU Member States (household and industry)
- graphs – gas prices (households and industry).

European Communities, Eurostat (Statistical Office of the EC)
ENERGY PRICES
Luxembourg: Office for Official Publications of the European Communities (annually)

Energy Prices 1980–1996, published in 1997, comprises statistical tables which give price indices in national currencies for:

- natural gas (households and industry)
- electricity (domestic and industrial)
- heating oil (household consumption)
- residual fuel oil (consumption by industry)
- premium gasoline
- premium unleaded gasoline
- diesel oil
- comparison between energy prices.

European Communities, Eurostat (Statistical Office of the EC)
ENERGY PRICES
Luxembourg: Office for Official Publications of the European Communities (annually)

The *Energy Prices* bulletin comprises tables which contain figures for:

- consumer prices for gas, electricity and oil in the EU Member States
- prices of energy in national currencies and ECU (European Currency Unit)
- comparative energy prices for the industrial and household sectors.

Detailed information on prices is published by the European Commission in:
Oil Price Bulletin (weekly)
Statistics in Focus for Gas and Electricity (biannually)

Gas Prices and Electricity Prices (annually)

European Communities, Eurostat (Statistical Office of the EC)
GAS PRICES
Luxembourg: Office for Official Publications of the European Communities (annually)

Gas Prices 1990–1996, published in 1997, comprises statistical tables. It gives the three price levels concerned, i.e. prices in national currencies, ECUs and purchasing power standard (annual value estimated for 1996).

Price indices in national currencies for:
• natural gas (domestic consumption)
• natural gas (industrial consumption)

Conversion factors

Graphs
• gas prices (domestic consumption)
• gas prices (industrial consumption)

European Communities, Eurostat (Statistical Office of the EC)
GAS PRICES – Price Systems
Luxembourg: Office for Official Publications of the European Communities (annually)

This bulletin gives information on:

• tariffs for large industrial customers and tariffs for small consumers
• price regulations in respect of gas
• taxation and the application of VAT (value-added tax).

International Monetary Fund (IMF)
INTERNATIONAL FINANCIAL STATISTICS YEARBOOK
Washington, D.C.: International Monetary Fund (annually)

This yearbook is updated by monthly bulletins. World tables are followed by country tables. Tables relevant to prices give figures for share prices, consumer prices and wholesale prices.

United Nations. Department for Economic and Social Information and Policy Analysis
STATISTICAL YEARBOOK
New York: United Nations (annually)

The *Statistical Yearbook* is international in scope. Countries are listed in alphabetical order. Figures for producer prices, consumer and wholesale prices are contained in the following tables:

• producer prices and wholesale prices
• consumer price index numbers.

Social Welfare

Official Publications

Central Statistics Office
STATISTICAL ABSTRACT
Dublin: Stationery Office (annually)

Each issue of the *Statistical Abstract* contains a section on social insurance, social services and pensions. The tables are supported by an explanatory text. Examples from the 1996 *Statistical Abstract* are listed below.

- expenditure on social welfare by scheme and financing, 1993–1995
- number of recipients of occupational injuries benefit, 1991–1995
- number of beneficiaries classified by type of allowance at 31 December, 1992–1995
- number of beneficiaries of deserted wife's benefit at 31 December, 1992–1995
- number of recipients of old age pensions by type of pension at 31 December 1995
- number of beneficiaries of supplementary welfare allowance by Health Board area at 31 December 1995
- particulars of families, children and cost of child benefit, 1990–1995

Central Statistics Office
ECONOMIC SERIES
Dublin: Stationery Office (monthly)

The *Economic Series* bulletin provides up-to-date information and five years' retrospection for a selection of 151 principal short-term economic series. Longer retrospection is given in each December issue.

Charts and graphs accompany the tables. The numbers pertaining to social welfare are as follows.

Monthly amount expended on:

9.12   Unemployment benefit
9.13   Unemployment assistance

Department of Social Welfare*
RATES OF PAYMENT FROM THE DEPARTMENT OF SOCIAL WELFARE
Dublin: Department of Social Welfare (annually)

This booklet gives the rates of payment for the various payments provided. The principal categories of payments are:

- pay-related social insurance (PRSI) (earnings thresholds for PRSI, contributions for self-employed people, voluntary contributions, PRSI contribution rates, etc.)
- unemployment payments (unemployment benefit, unemployment assistance, part-time job incentive scheme)
- family income support payments (child benefit, maternity benefit, health and safety benefit, family income supplement, supplementary welfare allowance, deserted wife's

allowance, lone parent's allowance, carer's allowance, widow's and widower's contributory pension, etc.)

- payments for incapacitated people (disability benefit, invalidity pension, blind person's pension)
- occupational injuries benefits payments (injury benefit, disablement benefit, unemployability supplement, medical care, etc.)
- payments for retired or elderly people (retirement pension, old-age contributory pension, pre-retirement allowance, old age non-contributory pension)
- extra benefits (butter vouchers, fuel allowance, natural gas allowance, free television licence, free telephone rental allowance, death grant, etc.)
- Health Board payments (blind welfare allowance, disabled person's maintenance allowance, income guidelines for medical card, charges in public hospitals, etc.)

* Since July 1997 Department of Social, Community and Family Affairs.

Department of Social Welfare*
STATISTICAL INFORMATION ON SOCIAL WELFARE SERVICES
Dublin: Department of Social Welfare (annually)

Statistical Information on Social Welfare Services 1995 was published in 1996 and is the thirteenth issue of this report. It contains comprehensive data on the services provided by what was then the Department of Social Welfare. The tables are grouped in the sections summarised below.

General
- expenditure on social welfare by programme
- expenditure on social welfare as a percentage of current Government expenditure
- number of recipients and beneficiaries of weekly social welfare payments 1985 to 1995
- number of recipients, adult dependants and child dependants of weekly social welfare payment
- number of recipients of social welfare payments by programme and county
- number of insured persons 1985–1995
- index of short-term rates of payment and consumer price index, 1985 to 1995
- index of rates of payment for the long-term unemployed and consumer price index 1985 to 1995

Old age
- expenditure on old age by payment type
- expenditure by type of pension
- number of recipients by type of pension 1985 to 1995
- number of recipients of old-age pensions by type of pension and county

Family income support
- expenditure on family income support by payment type
- expenditure on unmarried mother's allowance, lone parent's allowance
- expenditure on child benefit, 1985 to 1995
- number of recipients of deserted wife's benefit, deserted wife's allowance and prisoner's wife's allowance 1985 to 1995
- number of families receiving child benefit

Illness

- expenditure on illness payments by payment type
- number of recipients of illness payments by payment type
- occupational injuries benefits: number of recipients of injury benefit
- number of recipients of disability benefit and invalidity pension

Unemployment

- expenditure on unemployment payments by payment type, 1985 to 1995
- number of recipients of unemployment benefit and unemployment assistance on the last Friday of each month, 1995

Miscellaneous benefits and allowances

Management and financial statistics

* Since July 1997 Department of Social, Community and Family Affairs.

Publications: International Organisations

European Communities, Commission

SOCIAL PROTECTION IN THE MEMBER STATES OF THE EUROPEAN UNION – situation on 1 July (year)

Luxembourg: Office for Official Publications of the European Communities (annually)

The text in this report is tabulated to facilitate comparisons among the social security schemes in operation. The report contains information on:

- trends in social protection in the European Union
- structure and organisation of the health and welfare services in the EU Member States
- financing health and welfare services (contribution rates and membership ceiling)
- health care (legislation, eligibility, eligibility of citizens, hospital services, home help services, membership ceiling)
- sickness – cash benefits (legislation, maternity benefits, invalidity benefit, old age benefits, family benefits, unemployment benefits, etc.)
- employment injuries and occupational diseases (legislation, family benefits, unemployment benefit, social protection of unemployed persons, etc.)
- guaranteeing sufficient resources (i.e. minimum social insurance contributory schemes)
- social protection of self-employed people (special schemes for farmers and people in business).

European Communities, Eurostat (Statistical Office of the EC)

SOCIAL PROTECTION EXPENDITURE AND RECEIPTS

Luxembourg: Office for Official Publications of the European Communities (annually)

Social Protection Expenditure and Receipts 1980–1994 was published in 1996. The data on social protection expenditure and receipts for the Member States are drawn up according to the European system of integrated social protection statistics (ESSPROS), 1981 version. Summarised below are the main sections of this bulletin.

Summary tables
- social protection expenditure as % of Gross Domestic Product at market prices
- social protection current expenditure per head in ECUs
- social protection current expenditure per head in ECUs at constant 1985 prices
- social protection current expenditure per head in PPS
- social protection benefits by function as % of Gross Domestic Product
- social protection benefits by function as % of total benefits
- social protection current receipts by type as % of total receipts
- social protection current receipts by sector of origin as % of total receipts

Expenditure and receipts tables (in national currency and in ECUs)
- social protection benefits by function
- current expenditure on social protection by type
- social protection current receipts by type
- social protection current receipts by sector of origin

Economic and demographic indicators
- Gross Domestic Product at market prices (national currency)
- population
- ECU conversion rate
- PPS conversion rate
- consumer price indices in national currency (base 1985 = 100)
- consumer price indices in ECUs (base 1985 = 100)

European Communities, Eurostat (Statistical Office of the EC)
TAXES AND SOCIAL CONTRIBUTIONS
Luxembourg: Office for Official Publications of the European Communities (annually)

Taxes and Social Contributions 1983–1994 yearbook was published in 1996. It contains detailed information about the receipts of the Government sector (broken down in central government, local government and social security funds) from taxes and social contributions. Explanatory notes and methodology used precede the tables grouped in three sections as follows.

Comparative tables
- receipts of general Government and of the institutions of the EU from taxes and social contributions as % of GDP
- taxes and social contributions as % of GDP
- taxes and social contributions in ECUs per capita
- structure of receipts of general Government from taxes and social contributions as percentages
- taxes and social contributions as % of GDP per country

Country tables

Basic indicators
- Gross Domestic Product (GDP) at market prices
- price index of Gross Domestic Product (1990 = 100)
- total population

Organisation for Economic Co-operation and Development (OECD)
TAX/BENEFIT POSITION OF PRODUCTION WORKERS
Paris: OECD (annually)

This publication examines personal income taxes, employees' social security contributions and universal cash transfers received by family units at the average earnings level of workers in the manufacturing sector. Explanatory notes accompany the tables for each OECD member country in respect of:

- annual gross earnings
- income tax (single/widowed persons and married couples)
- standard reliefs
- allowances
- income levies (employer and employee contributions)
- social security contributions.

Tourism

Central Statistics Office
ECONOMIC SERIES
Dublin: Stationery Office (monthly)

The *Economic Series* bulletin provides up-to-date information and five years' retrospection for a selection of 151 principal short-term economic series. Longer retrospection is given in each December issue. Charts and graphs accompany the tables. The numbers pertaining to tourism are:

6.18   Overseas visitors to Ireland
6.19   Visits abroad by Irish residents

Central Statistics Office
STATISTICAL ABSTRACT
Dublin: Stationery Office (annually)

Each issue of the *Statistical Abstract* contains a section on tourism. The tables are supported by an explanatory text. Examples from the 1996 *Statistical Abstract* are listed below.

- visitors to Ireland – estimated expenditure and total international tourism and travel earnings
- overseas visitors to Ireland – estimated expenditure classified by area of residence and reason for journey
- overseas visitors to Ireland – estimated average length of stay (nights) classified by route of travel, area of residence and reason for journey
- overseas visits by Irish residents – estimated expenditure classified by reason of journey
- overseas visits by Irish residents – estimated average length of stay (nights) classified by route of travel and reason for journey
- total passenger movement by sea, rail, road and air classified by route of travel
- Bord Fáilte Éireann (Irish Tourist Board): income and expenditure

Central Statistics Office
STATISTICAL BULLETIN + Index
Dublin: Stationery Office (quarterly)

Statistics for tourism and travel are presented in each issue of the *Statistical Bulletin*. Tables give figures for:

- overseas visitors to Ireland – estimated number of overseas visits classified by route of travel, area of residence and reason for journey
- overseas visitors to Ireland – estimated average length of stay classified by route of travel, area of residence and reason for journey
- visits abroad by Irish residents – estimated number of visits classified by route of travel and reason for journey
- visits abroad by Irish residents – estimated average length of stay classified by route of travel and reason for journey

157

* tourism and travel – estimated earnings and expenditure.

Central Statistics Office
STATISTICAL RELEASES
Dublin: Central Statistics Office

Statistical Releases issued by the Central Statistics Office update the information and statistics in the *Statistical Bulletin*. The *Release* issued for tourism is:

Tourism and Travel (quarterly and annually).

Department of Foreign Affairs
DEVELOPMENTS IN THE EUROPEAN UNION
Dublin: Stationery Office (biannually)

In accordance with Section 5 of the 1972 European Communities Act, the Government is required to submit twice yearly to each House of the Oireachtas a report on the developments in the European Communities. Topics relevant to tourism include:

* Community Action Plan to assist tourism
* developments in the tourist industry.

Other Publications: Irish

Bord Fáilte Éireann – Irish Tourist Board
ANNUAL REPORT AND ACCOUNTS
Dublin: Bord Fáilte Éireann (annually)

Bord Fáilte Éireann was established under the Tourist Traffic Act, 1955. It works in close partnership with industry to maximise Ireland's revenue from tourism. By marketing Irish tourism abroad, the Bord also creates additional employment.

The Chairman's Statement comments on:
* the performance of Bord Fáilte
* marketing Irish tourism abroad
* work of the Regional Tourism Authorities
* co-operation of the Bord with other agencies to promote the tourist industry in Ireland.

The Director General's Review covers:
* performance of the tourist industry in Ireland
* the contribution of tourism to the Irish economy
* the Bord's marketing strategies and the travel trade
* creation and development of markets in Great Britain, Northern Ireland, Europe, North America and the rest of the world
* contribution of the airlines, i.e. Aer Lingus, Delta, World Airlines, Ryanair and other charter flights to tourism
* contribution of the cross-channel sea services
* investment in the tourist industry with funding from the European Regional Development Fund (ERDF)

- development of various facilities and leisure activities for tourists
- investment in various projects, such as accommodation, angling, cruising, coach tours, heritage sites.

The Annual Report also contains:
- figures for tourist numbers, revenue from tourism, foreign tourism revenue, employment, market performance, regional distribution of tourism revenue and Bord Fáilte budget allocation
- financial statements
- structure and organisation of Bord Fáilte.

Publications: International Organisations

European Communities, Eurostat (Statistical Office of the EC)
TOURISM: Annual Statistics
Luxembourg: Office for Official Publications of the European Communities (annually)

The yearbook *Tourism: Annual Statistics 1994* was published in 1997. Because statistical information collected at national level differs, data presented in the Eurostat *Tourism* yearbook are not always complete for all countries. Wherever available, the tables contain figures for the following.

Tourist accommodation
- hotels and similar establishments – national data
- hotels – regional data
- private tourist accommodation – regional data

Resident and non-resident guest flows in accommodation establishments

Non-resident guest flows in accommodation establishments

Accommodation capacity utilisation

Other tourist activities
- restaurants, public houses, travel agencies, car rentals, etc.

Employment in accommodation establishments and other tourist activities

Arrivals of non-resident visitors recorded at the external borders

Tourist expenditure

Trends in certain tourist consumer prices

Balance of payments
- travel – annual, quarterly, monthly data
- travel – geographical breakdown
- passenger transport – annual, quarterly, monthly data
- passenger transport – geographical breakdown

Organisation for Economic Co-operation and Development (OECD)
TOURISM POLICY AND INTERNATIONAL TOURISM IN OECD COUNTRIES
Paris: OECD (annually)

This report is prepared by the Tourism Committee, and provides information on:

- tourism in OECD member countries
- trends in national and international tourism
- tourist flows in OECD countries
- international tourism receipts and expenditure
- individual country data (tourist arrivals and nights spent in hotels and similar establishments, tourist receipts and expenditure)
- monthly hotel occupancy rates.

Most issues carry a special feature article such as 'Tourism strategies and rural development', 'Tourism and employment'.

Trade

Official Publications

Central Statistics Office
ECONOMIC SERIES
Dublin: Stationery Office (monthly)

The *Economic Series* bulletin provides up-to-date information and five years' retrospection for a selection of 151 principal short-term economic series. Longer retrospection is given in each December issue.

Charts and graphs accompany the tables. Listed below are the numbers pertaining to external trade.

Total trade
5.01	Imports
5.02	Exports
5.03	Trade surplus
5.04	Imports (seasonally adjusted)
5.05	Exports (seasonally adjusted)
5.06	Trade surplus (seasonally adjusted)
5.07	Imports from EU countries
5.08	Exports to EU countries

Categories of use
5.09	Imports of producers' capital goods ready for use
5.10	Imports of consumption goods ready for use
5.11	Imports of materials for further production
5.12	Exports of agricultural produce
5.13	Exports of industrial produce

Unit value and volume indices
5.14	Import price (unit value) index
5.15	Export price (unit value) index
5.16	Terms of trade index
5.17	Volume of imports index
5.18	Volume of imports index (SA)
5.19	Volume of exports index
5.20	Volume of exports index (SA)

(SA = seasonally adjusted)

Central Statistics Office
STATISTICAL ABSTRACT
Dublin: Stationery Office (annually)

Each issue of the *Statistical Abstract* contains a section on external trade. The tables are supported by an explanatory text. Examples from the 1996 *Statistical Abstract* are listed below.

- external trade

161

- external trade in each year 1933 to 1995
- imports by country of origin, 1990–1995
- exports by country of destination, 1990–1995
- imports/exports by SITC section and division of (Rev 3) 1994 and 1995
- distribution of imports according to main uses, 1990–1995
- distribution of exports by industrial origin, 1990–1995
- trade by areas, 1993–1995

Central Statistics Office
STATISTICAL BULLETIN + Index
Dublin: Stationery Office (quarterly)

External trade figures are published in each issue of the *Statistical Bulletin*. An explanatory text accompanies the tables which contain figures for:

- value of trade (£ million)
- volume, price and terms of trade indices
- trade by area (£ million)
- imports by main use
- exports by industrial origin
- trade by section of SITC (£ million).

Central Statistics Office
STATISTICAL RELEASES
Dublin: Central Statistics Office

Statistical Releases issued by the Central Statistics Office update the information and statistics in the *Statistical Bulletin*. The *Releases* issued for trade are:

Trade with non-EU countries – provisional (monthly)
Total external trade – provisional estimates (monthly).

Central Statistics Office
TRADE STATISTICS
Dublin: Stationery Office (monthly)

Explanatory notes and summary tables precede the detailed tables for foreign trade. Examples are listed below.

Summary tables
- summary of trade (imports/exports) 1961 onwards
- seasonally adjusted monthly value and volume indices of trade
- imports by main use
- imports by main use and area of origin
- exports by industrial origin
- exports by industrial origin and area of destination
- trade by area
- trade by area: percentage distribution
- trade by country

- trade by SITC section and division

Detailed tables
- trade by SITC division and country
- trade by country and SITC division
- imports and exports by SITC heading and country
- examples of imports/exports in the standard divisions: live animals, dairy products, fish, vegetable, feedingstuffs, cereals, beverages, tobacco, fuels, raw materials, vegetable and animal oils and fats, organic and inorganic chemicals, leather and rubber goods, textiles, iron and steel, non-ferrous metals, machinery and equipment, vehicles and transport equipment, furniture, travel goods, footwear, machinery specialised for specific industries.

The December issue of *Trade Statistics* contains the cumulative totals for the full year.

Department of Finance
ECONOMIC REVIEW AND OUTLOOK
Dublin: Stationery Office (annually)

The appendix in *Economic Review and Outlook* comprises statistical tables with comparative figures for approximately nine years. Tables relevant to trade are:

- value and volume of exports and imports
- sectoral origin of exports
- distribution of imports according to main use
- percentage distribution of trade by area.

Other Publications: Irish

An Bord Tráchtála – the Irish Trade Board*
ANNUAL REPORT AND ACCOUNTS
Dublin: An Bord Tráchtála (annually)

An Bord Tráchtála/the Irish Trade Board was established in September 1991 to combine the activities of the Irish Goods Council and Córas Tráchtála/Irish Export Board. It assists Irish firms to find markets for their products at home and abroad and provides information to overseas companies regarding the Irish market, products and services.

The Chairman's Statement comments on:

- the performance of Bord Tráchtála
- the Board's investment in marketing
- world trade flows
- Ireland's trade policy
- exports of Irish products and services
- performance of Irish companies abroad
- outlook for Irish merchandise in foreign markets.

The *Annual Report* also contains market reports for the United Kingdom, Germany, France, Netherlands, Belgium, Luxembourg, Italy, Spain, Portugal, Denmark, Finland, Norway, Sweden,

Central and Eastern Europe, North America, Latin American countries, selected Asian countries, Australia and New Zealand.

* Since July 1998 the functions of Bord Tráchtála have been absorbed by Enterprise Ireland.

An Bord Tráchtála – the Irish Trade Board*
ANNUAL REVIEW AND OUTLOOK
Dublin: An Bord Tráchtála (annually)

The Chairman's Statement and the Chief Executive's Statement comment on:

- services provided by the Board to companies and customers at home and abroad
- market promotional programmes
- performance and growth of Irish exports
- performance of indigenous companies
- the impact of trade globalisation.

The *Annual Review and Outlook* also contains:

- information on various markets
- information on specific sectors of the market
- review of specific companies
- outlook for Irish exports and business opportunities

* Since July 1998 the functions of Bord Tráchtála have been absorbed by Enterprise Ireland.

Publications: International Organisations

European Communities, Eurostat (Statistical Office of the EC)
EU EXTERNAL TRADE INDICES
Luxembourg: Office for Official Publications of the European Communities (annually)

Methodology, sources and abbreviations precede the graphs and statistical tables which are grouped in three sections summarised below.

SITC Rev. 3 – Standard International Trade Classification
- food and live animals
- beverages and tobacco
- chemicals and related products
- manufactured goods
- meat and meat preparations
- dairy products
- textile fibres
- coal, coke and briquettes
- petroleum and petroleum products
- vegetables and fruit
- sugar
- medical and pharmaceutical products
- fertilisers etc.

BEC – Broad Economic Categories
- food and beverages/primary
- food and beverages/primary/mainly for industry
- food and beverages/primary/mainly for household consumption
- consumer goods
- transport equipment
- fuels and lubricants/processed

NACE-CLIO R44 – General Industrial Classification of Economic Activities in the European Union used in the input/output tables
- agricultural, forestry and fishery products
- metal products
- electrical goods
- textiles and clothing
- motor vehicles etc.

Trade indices
- intra-EU
- extra-EU
- total trade
- exports – annual, quarterly and monthly indices

European Communities, Eurostat (Statistical Office of the EC)
EXTERNAL AND INTRA-EUROPEAN UNION TRADE – Statistical Yearbook
Luxembourg: Office for Official Publications of the European Communities (annually)

Notes and methodology employed precede the detailed tables which contain figures for:

- the European Union and world trade
- share of trade of the European Union, the United States and Japan
- trends in EU trade by partner country
- trends in extra-EU trade by product
- trends in intra-EU trade by product
- trade balances by Member State
- external trade figures for each Member State.

European Communities, Eurostat (Statistical Office of the EC)
EXTERNAL AND INTRA-EUROPEAN UNION TRADE – monthly statistics
Luxembourg: Office for Official Publications of the European Communities (monthly)

This bulletin mainly comprises statistical tables supported by graphs. Coverage includes the following.

Trends in European Union trade
- extra-EU trade by main partner
- extra-EU trade by main product
- extra-EU trade by Member State
- intra-EU trade by Member State
- extra-EU trade indices by partner country
- extra-EU trade indices by product

- intra-EU trade indices by product

European Union and world trade
- trends in world trade
- share of trade of the EU, the United States and Japan

European Union trading partners
- main EU trading partners
- yearly/monthly trends in EU trade by product
- geographical breakdown of EU trade by main product
- main EU trading partners by main product

Member States and EU trade
- trade balance by Member State
- intra/extra-EU trade by Member State
- breakdown by Member State of extra-EU trade by main partner country
- breakdown by Member State of goods traded intra-EU and extra-EU

External trade by Member States

EFTA external trade

European Communities, Eurostat (Statistical Office of the EC)
INTERNATIONAL TRADE IN SERVICES EU
Luxembourg: Office for Official Publications of the European Communities (annually)

International Trade in Services EU 1985–1994, published in 1996, is the first issue of a yearly publication. Data are presented according to the 5th edition of the IMF *Balance of Payments Manual*, 1993.

Detailed tables contain data for each EU Member State in respect of:

- services (communication services, financial services, insurance services, computer and information services, legal accounting and management consulting services, technical and engineering services, research and development, architectural and construction services, agricultural advisory services, mining and other technical services)
- current account transfers
- capital account transfers.

Food and Agriculture Organization (FAO)
TRADE YEARBOOK
Rome: FAO (annually)

The FAO *Trade Yearbook* covers approximately 160 countries. Commodity notes, quantity conversion factors, exchange rates and maritime freight rates for wheat precede the country tables arranged in four sections.

FAO indices of agricultural trade, by continent
Indices of volume, unit value and value of imports/exports of total agricultural products

Trade in agricultural products
Animal and dairy products, eggs, cereals, oil seeds, beverages, fruits, sugar, pulses, etc.

Trade in means of agricultural production
Tractors, farm machinery, fertilisers and pesticides.

Value of agricultural, fishery and forestry trade by country

International Monetary Fund (IMF)
DIRECTION OF TRADE STATISTICS YEARBOOK
Washington, D.C.: International Monetary Fund (annually + quarterly updates)

The *Direction of Trade Statistics* yearbook presents seven years' data for approximately 181 countries. It is updated by quarterly issues which cover approximately 152 countries.

The tables show trade flows and contain figures for imports and exports.

In the world section, countries are grouped as industrial countries, developing countries and other countries.

Individual countries follow the world section in alphabetical order.

Organisation for Economic Co-operation and Development (OECD)
MONTHLY STATISTICS OF FOREIGN TRADE: Series A (monthly)
FOREIGN TRADE BY COMMODITIES: Series B
FOREIGN TRADE BY COMMODITIES: Series C (annually in 5 volumes)
Paris: OECD

The monthly bulletin is an up-to-date source of data on the foreign trade of OECD member countries. The data, however, are less detailed than in the annual Series C bulletin which gives full details by commodity as well as by partner country.

Series A
Monthly Statistics of Foreign Trade comprises statistical tables arranged in four parts

Part 1
- foreign trade indicators (imports/exports)
- total trade of OECD countries
- trade of OECD country groupings by main region
- trade of OECD countries with NAFTA, with OECD–Europe, with
- non-OECD countries

Part 2
- volume and average value indices

Part 3
- trade by SITC sections

Part 4
- foreign trade of member countries by partner countries.

United Nations Conference on Trade and Development (UNCTAD)
HANDBOOK OF INTERNATIONAL TRADE AND DEVELOPMENT STATISTICS
New York: United Nations (annually)

The *Handbook of International Trade and Development Statistics 1995* was published in 1997. It is intended to provide a comprehensive collection of statistical data relevant to the analysis of world trade. The handbook is divided into seven parts and each part contains detailed tables.

Part 1
Value, growth and shares of world trade in current prices; trade balances; intra-trade by region

Part 2
Volume, unit value and terms of trade indices for developed and developing countries and territories by region and economic grouping; commodity price indices

Part 3
Network of world trade; summary by selected regions of origin and destination; export and import structure by selected commodity groups

Part 4
Export and import structure by commodity and by country; major exports of developing countries and territories by leading exporters

Part 5
Balance of payments, foreign direct investment, financial resource flows and external indebtedness

Part 6
Basic indicators of development

Part 7
Special studies

United Nations. Department for Economic and Social Information and Policy Analysis
INTERNATIONAL TRADE STATISTICS YEARBOOK (2 volumes)
New York: United Nations (annually)

The *International Trade Statistics Yearbook* covers 182 countries and provides the basic information for individual countries' external trade performances in terms of the overall trends in current value, as well as in volume and prices.

Volume 1 – Trade by country
Tables
- historical series – foreign trade (1959 to the current year)
- imports by broad economic category
- exports by industrial origin
- trade by principal countries of origin and last destination (value in thousand US dollars)
- imports of commodities (according to SITC Rev. 2)
- exports of commodities (according to SITC Rev. 2)

Volume 2 – Trade by commodity

United Nations. Department for Economic and Social Information and Policy Analysis
STATISTICAL YEARBOOK
New York: United Nations (annually)

The *Statistical Yearbook* is international in scope. Countries are listed in alphabetical order. Figures for foreign trade are contained in the following tables:

- international merchandise trade
- total imports and exports (value in million US dollars)
- world exports by commodity classes and by regions
- total imports and exports: index numbers (base year 1990 = 100).

World Trade Organization (WTO)
ANNUAL REPORT (2 volumes)
Geneva: World Trade Organization (annually)

The World Trade Organization (WTO) is the legal and institutional foundation of the multilateral trading system. It provides the principal contractual obligations determining how governments frame and implement domestic trade legislation and regulations. The WTO was established on 1 January 1995. At the end of July 1996 123 countries and territories were members of the WTO. It has superseded the General Agreement on Tariffs and Trade (GATT). The two volumes are summarised below.

Volume 1
This volume mainly comprises text supported by charts, graphs and tables. Coverage includes:

- world trade in 1995 and prospects for 1996
- the state of world trade, trade policy and the WTO
- trade policy developments
- trade and foreign direct investment
- WTO activities

Volume 2
This volume mainly comprises tables and charts. Figures are given for the following.
World trade in 1995
- growth in the volume of world merchandise exports and production by major product group (five-year period)
- growth in the value of world merchandise trade by region
- growth in the volume of world merchandise trade by region
- leading exporters and importers in world merchandise trade
- leading importers and exporters in world trade in commercial services

Selected long-term trends
- world merchandise exports, production and Gross Domestic Product (GDP)
- world merchandise trade and output by major product group
- leading exporters of manufactures
- leading importers of manufactures

Trade by region
- North America
- Latin America
- Western Europe

169

- Central and Eastern Europe, the Baltic States and the (CIS) transaction economies
- Africa
- Middle East
- Asia

Trade by sector
Food, fuels, iron and steel, chemicals, machinery and transport equipment, office machines and telecom equipment, automotive products, textiles, clothing, commercial services

Official Publications

Central Statistics Office
ECONOMIC SERIES
Dublin: Stationery Office (monthly)

The *Economic Series* bulletin provides up-to-date information and five years' retrospection for a selection of 151 principal short-term economic series. Longer retrospection is given in each December issue. Charts and graphs accompany the tables. Listed below are the numbers pertaining to transport.

Vehicle licensing
6.09   Private cars (new)
6.10   Private cars (second-hand)
6.11   Goods vehicles (new)
6.12   Goods vehicles (second-hand)
6.13   Tractors (new and second-hand)

Passenger movement by sea
6.14   Outward
6.15   Inward

Passenger movement by air (excluding internal and transit)
6.16   Outward
6.17   Inward

Central Statistics Office
ROAD FREIGHT TRANSPORT SURVEY
Dublin: Stationery Office (annually)

The *Road Freight Transport Survey 1994* was published in 1996. The scope of the survey and an analysis of goods vehicle activity in 1994 is followed by detailed tables. Examples are listed below.

- estimated transport activity classified by business of owner and main use of vehicle
- estimated transport activity classified by business of owner, length of haul and main use of vehicle
- estimated transport activity classified by region of origin and main use of vehicle
- estimated transport activity classified by internal and international journeys
- estimated transport activity classified by group of goods and main use of vehicle
- estimated transport activity classified by region of origin and region of destination

Central Statistics Office
STATISTICAL ABSTRACT
Dublin: Stationery Office (annually)

Each issue of the *Statistical Abstract* contains a section on motor vehicles, passenger road services, roads and road freight. Examples from the 1996 *Statistical Abstract* are listed below.

171

Motor vehicles

- mechanically propelled vehicles under current licence on 31 December 1995 and driving licences current on 31 December 1995, with comparative totals for 1990–1994
- new motor vehicles licensed for the first time in 1995
- new private cars licensed for the first time, 1991–1995
- new private cars licensed for the first time in 1995 classified by engine capacity in each motor taxation authority

Passenger road services

- scheduled omnibus passenger services, 1991–1995
- seating capacity of omnibus passenger vehicles under current licence in December, 1991–1995

Roads and road freight

- summary of Road Authority expenditure on public roads in 1993
- amounts expended by Road Authorities on maintenance and improvement of public roads in the year ended 31 December 1993
- mileage of public roads as at 31 December 1977
- Córas Iompair Éireann: consolidated balance sheet 1994 and 1995
- Córas Iompair Éireann: consolidated profit and loss account 1994 and 1995
- Iarnród Éireann: length of railway lines, 1991–1995
- Iarnród Éireann – Irish Rail: revenue and expenditure, 1994 and 1995
- Iarnród Éireann – Irish Rail: principal commodities conveyed by rail, 1991–1995
- Iarnród Éireann – Irish Rail: details of traffic conveyed by rail, 1991–1995

Air traffic and shipping

- Aer Lingus Group: consolidated balance sheets, years ending 31 December 1994 and 1995
- Aer Lingus Group: consolidated profit and loss accounts, years ending 31 December 1994 and 1995
- combined staff numbers of Aer Lingus plc and Aerlinte plc at 31 March of each year 1993–1995
- number and net tonnage of vessels registered at 31 December, 1993–1995
- arrivals of vessels and number of livestock handled at Irish ports, 1991–1995
- tonnage of goods handled at Irish ports, 1990–1995
- shipping casualties off the coast as notified under the Merchant Shipping Act, 1984 for 1993–1995

Central Statistics Office
STATISTICAL BULLETIN + Index
Dublin: Stationery Office (quarterly)

Statistics of port traffic are published annually in the *Statistical Bulletin*. The tables contain figures for:

- arrivals of trading and passenger vessels and weight of goods handled each year (eight-year period)
- number of arrivals and net register tonnage of trading and passenger vessels classified by Harbour Authority and by flag
- weight of goods handled classified by category of traffic
- details of roll-on/off traffic handled by each Harbour Authority

- weight of goods and number of livestock handled by each Harbour Authority
- weight of goods handled by each Harbour Authority classified by category of traffic.

A list of all the Harbour Authorities is included.

Central Statistics Office
STATISTICAL BULLETIN + Index
Dublin: Stationery Office (quarterly)

Each issue of the *Statistical Bulletin* has tables containing figures for transport as listed below:

- particulars of motor vehicles licensed for the first time
- air traffic statistics
- rail services – Iarnród Éireann
- passenger road services
- cross-border passenger movement
- passenger movement by sea.

Central Statistics Office
STATISTICAL RELEASES
Dublin: Stationery Office

Statistical Releases issued by the Central Statistics Office update the information and statistics in the *Statistical Bulletin*. The Releases issued for transport are:

- *Vehicle licensing – provisional results* (monthly)
- *Vehicle licensing – final detailed results* (monthly)
- *Vehicle licensing* (annually)
- *Statistics of port traffic* (annually).

Only the activity of trading vessels, car ferries and other passenger vessels is covered in the series. Private fishing vessels and yachts are excluded.

Department of Foreign Affairs
DEVELOPMENTS IN THE EUROPEAN UNION
Dublin: Stationery Office (biannually)

In accordance with section 5 of the 1972 European Communities Act, the Government is required to submit twice yearly to each House of the Oireachtas a report on the developments in the European Communities. Topics relevant to transport include:

- efficient pricing in transport
- air traffic management
- Council Directives on maritime transport
- air transport, licensing of air carriers
- air fares and rates
- road transport – Regulations and Directives.

Department of Transport, Energy and Communications*

ANNUAL REPORT AND FINANCIAL STATEMENTS
Dublin: Department of Transport, Energy and Communications (annually)

The Secretary's Review assesses the role of the Department of Enterprise, Trade and Employment and the performance of the transport, energy and communications sectors.

Transport sector – new developments
- in 1996 the European Commission was given a mandate to open air transport negotiations with the associated countries of Central Europe
- negotiations commenced with the United States on a common aviation area
- Aer Rianta development plans
- performance of Aer Lingus and restructuring programme
- progress on the future of railways in Europe
- progress on the Dublin Light Rail Transit System (LUAS)
- mainline and suburban rail investment
- public transport contracts
- performance criteria for CIE services
- road haulage and political agreements on international bus operations

Energy sector – new developments
- progress on common rules for the Internal Market in gas
- political agreement on the ratification by the Communities of the Energy Charter Treaty
- adoption of the Directive establishing common rules for the Internal Market in electricity
- production of electricity, peat and gas
- oil supplies and the Whitegate Oil Refinery
- energy issues relating to climate change

Communications – new developments
- new developments in the telecommunications and postal sectors

Reviews of the undermentioned sectors follow.

Transport
- Aer Lingus – performance of the airline, restructuring of the company, State aid, TEAM Aer Lingus, etc.
- civil aviation and international developments in air services, passenger traffic, etc.
- airports – services and performance
- travel trade information
- public transport
- Córas Iompair Éireann (CIE) – restructuring the Board of CIE, performance measurement, public transport contracts, State subvention, etc.
- road haulage and road transport legislation
- transport policy developments in the European Union

Energy
- restructuring of the electricity industry, rationalisation package for the Electricity Supply Board (ESB)
- peat, natural gas, oil – supplies

Communications
- Telecommunication services, Telecom Éireann, postal services, An Post, radio and television licences, etc.

The Annual Report also includes the organisational structure of the Department.

* Since July 1997 Department of Enterprise, Trade and Employment.

Department of Transport, Energy and Communications*
IRISH BULLETIN OF VEHICLE AND DRIVER STATISTICS
Shannon, Co. Clare: Department of the Environment (annually)

This bulletin comprises statistical tables. Examples are listed below.

- vehicle statistics (25-year period) for private cars, motor cycles, goods vehicles, tractors, public service vehicles, etc.
- number of mechanically propelled vehicles by taxation class at 31 December
- number of private cars by cubic capacity of engine
- number of goods vehicles by unladen weight
- number of private cars and goods vehicles in each licensing authority area
- number of vehicles by taxation class in each licensing authority area
- number of tractors by make in each licensing authority area
- number of vehicles by taxation class and type of fuel
- age of private cars by cubic capacity
- age of goods vehicles
- number of new vehicles first licensed in each licensing authority area (ten-year period)
- vehicle testing results for heavy goods vehicles, trailers, buses and ambulances by county and county borough for the year ended 31 December...
- list of most common defects by category of vehicles, for year ended 31 December...
- pass rates by driving centre

* Since July 1997 Department of Enterprise, Trade and Employment.

Other Publications: Irish

Aer Lingus Group plc
ANNUAL REPORT AND CONSOLIDATED ACCOUNTS
Dublin: Aer Lingus (annually)

Aer Lingus was incorporated in 1936 as a State enterprise. In 1993 the company was restructured into Aer Lingus plc.

The Chairman's Statement reviews:

- main developments in the airline industry
- deregulation of the aviation markets
- performance of the Aer Lingus Group.

The Chief Executive's Review covers:

- business plans being pursued by the Group

- expansion of the company's business
- financial performance of the company
- operating profits and shareholders' funds
- performance of Group's passenger services – transatlantic, domestic, United Kingdom and European
- performance of the cargo division
- performance of its subsidiaries, i.e. TEAM Aer Lingus, Futura, Airmotive Ireland, SRS Aviation Ireland.

Aer Rianta – Irish Airports
ANNUAL REPORT AND ACCOUNTS
Dublin: Aer Rianta (annually)

Aer Rianta is a public limited company incorporated under the Companies Acts. It manages and develops Dublin, Shannon and Cork Airports. The Chairman's Statement and the Chief Executive's Review cover:

- performance of Aer Rianta and Aer Rianta International
- summary of the financial results of the company
- capital investment and new developments in progress at the three airports
- passenger traffic statistics and cargo-handling operations
- duty-free sales
- airport charges.

The Annual Report also includes the organisation and structure of the Board.

Córas Iompair Éireann (CIE)
GROUP ANNUAL REPORT AND FINANCIAL STATEMENTS
Dublin: Córas Iompair Éireann (annually)

Córas Iompair Éireann is the principal authority for the provision of public transport in Ireland. It is also a holding company and has three subsidiary companies, i.e. Bus Éireann–Irish Bus, Bus Átha Cliath–Dublin Bus and Iarnród Éireann–Irish Rail.
The Chairman's Statement gives a brief account of the Group's operations, performance, quality of service, investment programme, etc.

The *Annual Report* also contains:

- financial results by business sector, i.e. railway, road freight, road passenger
- State grants
- EU Regulations governing State aid to transport undertakings
- figures for operating costs.

Dublin Port
DUBLIN PORT FACT SHEET
Dublin: Dublin Port (annually)

The *Fact Sheet* has information on:

- RoRo and LoLo facilities available at Dublin Port
- liquid bulk facilities
- dry bulk facilities
- break-bulk facilities
- pilotage and towage facilities
- cranes – capacity and operations
- oil bunkering and warehousing facilities
- passenger services
- port statistics for the current and previous year
- forthcoming events.

Dublin Port

REPORT AND ACCOUNTS

Dublin: Dublin Port (annually)

Dublin Port's principal function is the management of the Port of Dublin. The Chairman's Report gives a review of:

- port traffic
- cargo throughput
- RoRo trade and the LoLo services at the terminals
- passenger services provided by the ferries
- freight services provided by the merchant ferries
- capital investment in developing Dublin Port.

National Roads Authority

ANNUAL REPORT AND ACCOUNTS

Dublin: National Roads Authority (annually)

The National Roads Authority was established as an independent statutory body under the Roads Act 1993 with effect from 1 January 1994. Its primary functions are:

- the provision of a safe and efficient network of national roads
- adequate provision of traffic signs and signals
- maintenance works and improvements on national roads
- preparing medium-term plans for developing the national road network
- making toll schemes.

The Chairman's Statement comments on:

- the activities, achievements and performance of the Authority
- accident prevention measures
- road traffic safety
- programme of projects.

The Financial Statement contains:

- Report of the Comptroller and Auditor General
- accounting policies of the Authority
- income and expenditure accounts

- balance sheet
- cashflow statement.

Publications: International Organisations

Organisation for Economic Co-operation and Development (OECD)
MARITIME TRANSPORT
Paris: OECD (annually)

Maritime Transport 1995, published in 1997, is divided into three parts. The text is supported by tables, charts and graphs and has information on:

- international shipping developments
- new developments in shipping policy outside the OECD area
- developments in OECD member countries
- developments in other intergovernmental organisations
- commercial developments in world shipping
- trends in international trade
- demand for shipping services
- supply of shipping services
- the freight market.

United Nations Conference on Trade and Development (UNCTAD)
REVIEW OF MARITIME TRANSPORT
New York: United Nations (annually)

The *Review of Maritime Transport 1997* comprises text supported by charts, graphs and tables. It is divided into the seven chapters summarised below.

Chapter 1: Development of international seaborne trade
- world economic background
- world seaborne trade

Chapter 2: Development of the world fleet
- structure of the world fleet
- ownership of the world fleet
- the 35 most important maritime countries and territories
- major open registries
- shipbuilding, second-hand market and demolition

Chapter 3: Productivity of the world fleet and the supply and demand situation in world shipping
- comparison of cargo turnover and fleet ownership
- estimate of tons and ton miles per cwt
- supply and demand in world shipping

Chapter 4: Freight markets
- freight market rates of major liner trades: TransPacific, TransAtlantic, and Europe–Asia
- liner freight index
- liner freight rates as a percentage of prices for selected commodities
- containership charter market

- dry bulk freight market
- oil and oil products seaborne freight market
- estimates of total freight costs in the world

Chapter 5: Port development
- container port traffic
- institutional restructuring in ports
- port performance
- port terminal security
- ship-to-shore crane orders

Chapter 6: Trade and transport efficiency
- trade efficiency
- multimodal transport and technological developments
- information technology in transport

Chapter 7: Review of regional developments: small island developing countries
- economic background
- costs of transport
- overview of the current situation in shipping

United Nations. Department for Economic and Social Information and Policy Analysis
STATISTICAL YEARBOOK
New York: United Nations (annually)

The *Statistical Yearbook* is international in scope. Countries are listed in alphabetical order. Figures for transport are contained in the following tables:

- railways: length of railways and number of passengers
- motor vehicles in use
- merchant shipping: fleets
- international maritime transport
- civil aviation.

United Nations. Economic Commission for Europe (ECE)
ANNUAL BULLETIN OF TRANSPORT STATISTICS FOR EUROPE AND NORTH AMERICA
Geneva: United Nations (annually)

This bulletin comprises statistical tables. Examples are as follows.

- population and area of country
- consumption of energy by transport sector
- road traffic accidents involving personal injury
- road network at end of year
- passenger traffic and transport
- national freight transport by ranges of distance
- roads – length of roads and expenditure on roads
- new vehicles registered during the year
- total and international road traffic and transport

- inland waterways – length and carrying capacity
- freight transport on international rivers e.g. Rhine and Danube
- goods loaded and unloaded at sea ports
- length of oil pipelines
- various modes of transport of goods and commodity groups

Author Index

Title Index

187

Subject Index